The
HAROLD ARLEN
Songbook

Edited by David Bickman

Published by
MPL COMMUNICATIONS, INC.

Exclusively distributed by
HAL LEONARD PUBLISHING CORPORATION
Winona, MN 55987   Milwaukee, WI 53213

ISBN 0-88188-425-1

Despite the fact that he has created an extraordinary number of classic songs (some often mistaken for folk songs), Harold Arlen, unlike his songs, needs an introduction.

For decades he has pretty much eluded the public eye; a cursory scanning of the table of contents of this musico-lyrical treasury should prove to be a revelation. It may even elicit a response in the form of a question to which the composer has been subjected for years: "You wrote that, too?" Consider just a few and consider, too, the versatility, the wit, the pathos, the form (rarely that of the standard 32-bar popular song), the poetry: OVER THE RAINBOW, STORMY WEATHER (published here for the first time in its complete form), GET HAPPY, BLUES IN THE NIGHT, COME RAIN OR COME SHINE — the temptation is to go on and on, but the songs sing for themselves, rich in the joy of discovery and rediscovery.

Harold Arlen was born in Buffalo on February 15, 1905. His father was a cantor and provided his earliest musical experiences. At seven he sang in his father's choir; two years later he began piano lessons, working his way up to the more secular Etudes of Chopin. But then at the age of twelve, he discovered jazz – Chopin's loss, our gain. Before long the cantor's son formed his own band, The Snappy Trio; he was the pianist-vocalist and devised the jazzy arrangements. To his parents' dismay, the Trio performed in Buffalo's tenderloin as well as on the lake boats plying the waters between Buffalo and Toronto. Successful, the Trio expanded into a quintet, The Southbound Shufflers, and to his parents' further consternation, young Hyman (as he was then known) dropped out of high school, a victim of history, mathematics and Latin.

But his musical talents received high marks and he was asked to join one of the most successful local bands, The Buffalodians, as vocalist, pianist and arranger. With this group, in mid-Jazz Age Arlen moved into the big time: New York. Eventually he left the band to write arrangements (for Fletcher Henderson, among others), then he worked as a single (vocal and piano) in vaudeville and, ultimately, he was cast in a singing role in a Broadway musical, Vincent Youmans' GREAT DAY. By the time the show opened, Arlen was long gone.

Youmans discovered that his would-be vocalist could read and write music and drafted him as a kind of musical secretary. Then one day the rehearsal pianist for the dancers called in sick and Arlen filled in. During the frequent waits, he played around with the dancers' "pickup" or vamp, the bar or two intro to their cues. As the day progressed, the little snippet evolved into a full-fledged song, to everyone's delight. One admirer, aspiring songwriter Harry Warren, then working for a publisher as a song-plugger, said to Arlen, "I know just the guy to write this up."

He turned out to be Ted Koehler and the dancers' former vamp emerged as GET HAPPY, Harold Arlen's first professional song. It was a tremendous hit in 1930 (and has been around ever since) and sprung him out of a performing career. The song's popularity led to an invitation to write for Harlem's celebrated Cotton Club Revues, resulting in several classics, among them STORMY WEATHER, which in turn led to his first film contract and yet another classic, LET'S FALL IN LOVE.

Many believe that Arlen's relative anonymity can be attributed to a long (and successfully productive) sojourn in California, where he remained for nearly two decades, from the mid-thirties, writing for the screen. There were occasional excursions to New York to work on Broadway, but his Hollywood residence confined him to the background while the stars and starlets shone up front.

This genuinely shy and modest great man did not mind. It was a good life, reasonably tension-free, and he and his beautiful wife, Anya, enjoyed the languid pleasures of Beverly Hills, partying with their friends: the Gershwins, Jerome Kern, Irving Berlin, Warren, et al. Meanwhile, Harold Arlen quietly accumulated one of the most impressive catalogs in the history of American popular song, not merely lucrative Hit Parade material (plenty of those), but evergreens — songs that have long outlived their original films and shows.

What makes this Arlen treasury so priceless is that it collects virtually all the Arlen classics (more are being discovered as time goes by); it also returns out-of-print gems back into print and, as an added plus, brings together many beloved Arlen rarities, even a few never before published songs. Notable among these is the haunting I HAD A LOVE ONCE, words and music by Harold Arlen, one of the last completed songs before his retirement. This unique volume illuminates the extraordinary artistry of Harold Arlen — an instantaneous collector's item!

Edward Jablonski

Mr. Jablonski is the author of **HAROLD ARLEN: HAPPY WITH THE BLUES, ENCYCLOPEDIA OF AMERICAN MUSIC** and **GERSHWIN** among others, and co-author of **THE GERSHWIN YEARS.**

THE HAROLD ARLEN SONGBOOK

SONG		SHOW/FILM
178	Ac-cent-tchu-ate The Positive	*Here Come The Waves (film)*
148	Ain' It De Truth?	*Jamaica*
186	Any Place I Hang My Hat Is Home	*St. Louis Woman*
64	As Long As I Live	*Cotton Club Parade 1934*
27	Between The Devil And The Deep Blue Sea	*Rhythmania*
124	Blues In The Night	*Blues In The Night (film)*
100	Buds Won't Bud	*Hooray For What*
254	Cocoanut Sweet	*Jamaica*
190	Come Rain Or Come Shine	*St. Louis Woman*
116	Ding-Dong! The Witch Is Dead	*The Wizard Of Oz (film)*
236	Dissertation On The State Of Bliss (Love And Learn)	*The Country Girl (film)*
250	Don't Like Goodbyes	*House Of Flowers*
104	Down With Love	*Hooray For What*
166	Eagle And Me, The	*Bloomer Girl*
160	Evelina	*Bloomer Girl*
80	Fancy Meeting You	*Stage Struck (film)*
214	For Every Man There's A Woman	*Casbah (film)*
60	Fun To Be Fooled	*Life Begins At 8:40*
23	Get Happy	*Nine-Fifteen Revue*
88	God's Country	*Hooray For What*
268	Goose Never Be A Peacock	*Saratoga*
145	Happiness Is A Thing Called Joe	*Cabin In The Sky (film)*
54	Happy As The Day Is Long	*Cotton Club Parade 1933*
284	Happy With The Blues	
137	Hit The Road To Dreamland	*Star Spangled Rhythm (film)*
211	Hooray For Love	*Casbah (film)*
229	House Of Flowers	*House Of Flowers*
30	I Gotta Right To Sing The Blues	*Earl Carroll's Vanities 1932*
298	I Had A Love Once	
194	I Had Myself A True Love	*St. Louis Woman*
244	I Never Has Seen Snow	*House Of Flowers*
204	I Wonder What Became Of Me	*St. Louis Woman*
38	I've Got The World On A String	*Cotton Club Parade 1932*
120	If I Only Had A Brain	*The Wizard Of Oz (film)*
57	Ill Wind	*Cotton Club Parade 1934*
96	In The Shade Of The New Apple Tree	*Hooray For What*
208	It Was Written In The Stars	*Casbah (film)*
44	It's Only A Paper Moon	*The Great Magoo*

SONG	SHOW/FILM
72 Last Night When We Were Young	
52 Let's Fall In Love	*Let's Fall In Love (film)*
67 Let's Take A Walk Around The Block	*Life Begins At 8:40*
174 Let's Take The Long Way Home	*Here Come The Waves (film)*
140 Life's Full Of Consequence	*Cabin In the Sky (film)*
151 Like A Straw In The Wind	
257 Little Drops Of Rain	*Gay Purr-ee (film)*
171 Lullaby	*St. Louis Woman*
232 Man That Got Away, The	*A Star Is Born (film)*
92 Moanin' In The Mornin'	*Hooray For What*
276 Money Cat, The	*Gay Purr-ee (film)*
286 Morning After, The	
154 My Shining Hour	*The Sky's The Limit (film)*
156 One For My Baby	*The Sky's The Limit (film)*
182 Out Of This World	*Out Of This World (film)*
112 Over The Rainbow	*The Wizard Of Oz (film)*
272 Paris Is A Lonely Town	*Gay Purr-ee (film)*
301 Promise Me Not To Love Me	
260 Push De Button	*Jamaica*
163 Right As The Rain	*Bloomer Girl*
34 Satan's Li'l Lamb	*Americana*
294 Silent Spring, The	
240 Sleepin' Bee, A	*House Of Flowers*
290 So Long, Big Time!	
48 Stormy Weather	*Cotton Club Parade 1933*
132 That Old Black Magic	*Star Spangled Rhythm (film)*
281 That's A Fine Kind O' Freedom	
264 There's A Sweet Wind Blowin' My Way	
129 This Time The Dream's On Me	*Blues In The Night (film)*
222 Today I Love Ev'rybody	*The Farmer Takes A Wife (film)*
41 Wail Of The Reefer Man, The	*Cotton Club Parade 1932*
217 What's Good About Goodbye?	*Casbah (film)*
109 When The Sun Comes Out	
84 When The Wind Blows South	
220 Who Will It Be When The Time Comes?	*Down Among The Sheltering Palms (film)*
226 With The Sun Warm Upon Me	*The Farmer Takes A Wife (film)*
200 Woman's Prerogative, A	*St. Louis Woman*
76 You're The Cure For What Ails Me	*The Singing Kid (film)*

THE WORKS OF HAROLD ARLEN

The following is a complete and, it is hoped, accurate listing of the compositions of Harold Arlen, both published and unpublished, including those published under the name of Harold Arluck. The motion pictures are followed by the month and year of the film's release. The stage productions are followed by their opening dates. All of the songs written for a particular film or production are listed, whether or not they appeared in the final version. Published songs are indicated with an asterisk (*). Songs included in this volume are indicated with two asterisks (**). Songs that are receiving their first publication in this volume are indicated with three asterisks (***).

1924

My Gal, Won't You Come Back To Me? (My Gal, My Pal) (lyric: Hyman Cheiffetz)
I Never Knew What Love Could Do (lyric: Hyman Cheiffetz)

1925

Easy Strain (lyric: Phil Shapiro)
I Want Your Kisses If You Want My Kisses (lyric: Phil Shapiro)

1926

*Minor Gaff (Blues Fantasy) (instrumental by Harold Arluck & Dick George)

1927

*Buffalo Rhythm (instrumental by Harold Arluck, Ivan Beaty, & Marvin Smolev)

1928

*Rhythmic Moments (for solo piano)
Jungaleena (lyric: Herb Magdison & James Cavanaugh)

1929

*The Album Of My Dreams (lyric: Lou Davis)
Can't Be Bothered With No One But You (lyric: Charles Tobias)
Heap O' Misery (lyric: Ted Koehler)
*Rising Moon (lyric: Jack Ellis)
That's What I Call Love (lyric: Jack Ellis)
*Gladly (lyric: Ted Koehler)
Who Could Say No? (lyric: Ted Koehler)
Bring Him Back Here (lyric: Lou Davis)

1930

Shaking The African (lyric: Ted Koehler)
NINE-FIFTEEN REVUE (opened February 11, 1930)
Lyrics by Ted Koehler
Gee It's So Good, It's Too Bad
**Get Happy
*You Wanted Me, I Wanted You
EARL CARROLL'S VANITIES OF 1930 (opened July 1, 1930)
Lyrics by Ted Koehler
*Contagious Rhythm
*Hittin' The Bottle
*The March Of Time
*One Love
*Out Of A Clear Blue Sky
BROWN SUGAR (opened 1930)
Lyrics by Ted Koehler
*Linda
*Song Of The Gigolo

1931

Ha-Ha-Ha (Gang Song) (lyric: Ted Koehler)
*Tell Me With A Love Song (lyric: Ted Koehler)

YOU SAID IT (opened January 19, 1931)
Lyrics by Jack Yellen
 *If He Really Loves Me
 *It's Different With Me
 *Learn To Croon
 *Sweet And Hot
  They Learn About Women From Me
 *What Do We Care?
  What'd We Come To College For?
 *While You Are Young
 *You'll Do
 *You Said It

RHYTHMANIA (opened March, 1931)
Lyrics by Ted Koehler
**Between The Devil And The Deep Blue Sea
  Breakfast Dance
 *I Love A Parade
 *Kickin' The Gong Around
 *'Neath The Pale Cuban Moon
  Trickeration

1932

*The Song That Makes Me Blue (lyric: Jack Yellen)
*I Forgive You (lyric: Jack Yellen)
*Y' Got Me, Baby (lyric: Jack Yellen)
*Stepping Into Love (lyric: Ted Koehler)
*Music, Music, Everywhere But Not A Song In My Heart (lyric: Ted Koehler)
*Another Night Alone (lyric: Ted Koehler)

EARL CARROLL'S VANITIES OF 1932 (opened September 27, 1932)
Lyrics by Ted Koehler
**I Gotta Right To Sing The Blues
 *Rockin' In Rhythm

AMERICANA (opened October 5, 1932)
**Satan's Li'l Lamb (lyric: E.Y. Harburg & John Mercer)

COTTON CLUB PARADE (21st Edition) (opened October 23, 1932)
Lyrics by Ted Koehler
 *Harlem Holiday
 *In The Silence Of The Night
**I've Got The World On A String
 *Minnie The Moocher's Wedding Day
 *That's What I Hate About Love
**The Wail Of The Reefer Man
 *You Gave Me Ev'rything But Love

GEORGE WHITE'S MUSIC HALL VARIETIES (opened November 22, 1932)
  Cabin In The Cotton (lyric: Irving Caesar & George White)
 *Two Feet In Two-Four Time (lyric: Irving Caesar)

THE GREAT MAGOO (opened December 2, 1932)
**It's Only A Paper Moon (lyric: Billy Rose & E.Y. Harburg)

1933

*Shame On You (lyric: Edward Heyman)

COTTON CLUB PARADE (22nd Edition)
Lyrics by Ted Koehler
 *Get Yourself A New Broom (And Sweep The Blues Away)
**Happy As The Day Is Long
 *Raisin' The Rent
**Stormy Weather

1934

LET'S FALL IN LOVE (released January, 1934)
Lyrics by Ted Koehler
  Breakfast Ball
**Let's Fall In Love
 *Love Is Love Anywhere
  She's Not The Type
 *This Is Only The Beginning

COTTON CLUB PARADE (24th Edition)
Lyrics by Ted Koehler
**As Long As I Live
 *Breakfast Ball
 *Here Goes
**Ill Wind (You're Blowin' Me No Good)
 *Primitive Prima Donna

LIFE BEGINS AT 8:40 (opened August 27, 1934)
Lyrics by Ira Gershwin & E.Y. Harburg
  All The Elks and Masons
  C'est La Vie
**Fun To Be Fooled
  I Couldn't Hold My Man
  I Knew Him When
  I'm A Collector Of Moonbeams
  I'm Not Myself
  It Was Long Ago
**Let's Take A Walk Around The Block
  Life Begins
  Life Begins At City Hall
  My Paramount-Publix-Roxy Rose
  Quartet Erotica
 *Shoein' The Mare
  Spring Fever
  Things
  Weekend Cruise (Will You Love Me Monday Morning As You Did On Friday Night?)
 *What Can You Say In A Love Song?
 *You're A Builder Upper

1935

**Last Night When We Were Young (lyric: E.Y. Harburg)

GENERAL MOTORS SYMPHONY HOUR (radio broadcast - December, 1935)
  Mood In Six Minutes (orchestrated by Robert Russell Bennett)

1936

STRIKE ME PINK (released January, 1936)
Lyrics by Lew Brown
 *Calabash Pipe
 *First You Have Me High (Then You Have Me Low)
 *The Lady Dances
 *Shake It Off (With Rhythm)

THE SINGING KID (released April, 1936)
Lyrics by E.Y. Harburg
  Four Fugitives From A Bolero Chain Gang
  Here's Looking At You
 *I Love To Sing-a
  My, How This Country Has Changed
 *Save Me, Sister
**You're The Cure For What Ails Me

STAGE STRUCK (released September, 1936)
Lyrics by E.Y. Harburg
**Fancy Meeting You
 *In Your Own Quiet Way
  The New Parade
  Why Can't I Remember Your Name?
  You're Kinda Grandish

GOLD DIGGERS OF 1937 (released December, 1936)
Lyrics by E.Y. Harburg
  Hush Ma Mouth
 *Let's Put Our Heads Together
  Life Insurance Song
 *Speaking Of The Weather
THE SHOW IS ON (opened December 25, 1936)
  Song Of The Woodman (lyric: E.Y. Harburg)

  How's By You (lyric: E.Y. Harburg)
  I'll Thank You To Stay Out Of My Dreams (lyric: E.Y. Harburg)
***When The Wind Blows South (lyric: E.Y. Harburg)

1937

  It's A Long, Long Way To Broadway (lyric: E.Y. Harburg)
  The Peter Pan Of Tin Pan Alley (lyric: E.Y. Harburg)
ARTISTS AND MODELS (released August, 1937)
 *Public Melody Number One (lyric: E.Y. Harburg)
HOORAY FOR WHAT! (opened December 1, 1937)
Lyrics by E.Y. Harburg
 **Buds Won't Bud
 **Down With Love
  A Fashion Girl
 **God's Country
  Hero Ballet
  Hooray For What?
  I Click The Heel And I Kiss the Hand
 *I've Gone Romantic On You
 **In The Shade Of The New Apple Tree
 *Life's A Dance
 **Moanin' In The Mornin'
  Napoleon's A Pastry
  That Night Of The Embassy Ball
  Vive For Geneva

1938

 *Love's A Necessary Thing (lyric: Ted Koehler)

1939

 *Let's Hit The Nail On The Head (lyric: Ted Koehler)
 *You've Got Me Sittin' On The Fence (lyric: Ted Koehler)
LOVE AFFAIR (released March, 1939)
 *Sing, My Heart (lyric: Ted Koehler)
THE WIZARD OF OZ (released August, 1939)
Lyrics by E.Y. Harburg
 **Ding-Dong! The Witch Is Dead
  Follow The Yellow Brick Road
 **If I Only Had A Brain (A Heart; The Nerve)
 *If I Were King Of The Forest
 *The Jitterbug
 *Lullaby League And Lollypop Guild
 *The Merry Old Land Of Oz
 *Munchkinland
 *Optimistic Voices (co-composer: Herbert Stothart)
 **Over The Rainbow
 *We're Off To See The Wizard
AT THE CIRCUS (released November, 1939)
Lyrics by E.Y. Harburg
 *Lydia The Tattooed Lady
  Step Up And Take A Bow
  Swingali
 *Two Blind Loves
GOOD NEWS (radio program - December, 1939)
 *American Minuet

1940

  Lonesome And Low (lyric: Ted Koehler)
**Like A Straw In The Wind (lyric: Ted Koehler) (note: first published 1962)

1941

**When The Sun Comes Out (lyric: Ted Koehler)

AMERICANEGRO SUITE (for voices and piano)
Lyrics by Ted Koehler
  *Big Time Comin'
  *I Got Dat Feelin'
  *I'm Here Lawd
  *Little Ace O' Spades
  *Reverend Johnson's Dream
  *Where Is Dis Road A-leadin' Me To?

BLUES IN THE NIGHT (released December, 1941)
Lyrics by Johnny Mercer
**Blues In The Night
 *Hang On To Your Lids, Kids
 *Says Who, Says You, Says I!
**This Time The Dream's On Me

1942

 *Life Could Be A Cakewalk With You (lyric: Ted Koehler)
  Unusual Weather (lyric: E.Y. Harburg)
 *The Moment I Laid Eyes On You (lyric: Ted Koehler)

CAPTAINS OF THE CLOUDS (released February, 1942)
 *Captains Of The Clouds (lyric: Johnny Mercer)

RIO RITA (released May, 1942)
Lyrics by E.Y. Harburg
  A Couple Of Caballeros
 *Long Before You Came Along
  Poor Whippoorwill

STAR SPANGLED RHYTHM (released December, 1942)
Lyrics by Johnny Mercer
  He Loved Me Till The All Clear Came
**Hit The Road To Dreamland
 *I'm Doing If For Defense
  Let's Go Sailor (Shore Leave)
 *Old Glory
 *On The Swing Shift
 *Sharp As A Tack
  A Sweater, A Sarong, And A Peek-A-Boo Bang
**That Old Black Magic

1943

 *If That's Propaganda (lyric: Ira Gershwin & E.Y. Harburg)

THEY GOT ME COVERED (released March, 1943)
 *Palsy Walsy (lyric: Johnny Mercer)

CABIN IN THE SKY (released May, 1943)
Lyrics by E.Y. Harburg
**Ain' It De Truth?
**Happiness Is A Thing Called Joe
  Jezebel Jones
**Life's Full Of Consequence
  Li'l Black Sheep
  Petunia's Prayer
  Some Folks Work (Is You Man Or Mule?)

THE SKY'S THE LIMIT (released September, 1943)
Lyrics by Johnny Mercer
  Hangin' On To You
 *Harvey, The Victory Garden Man
 *A Lot In Common With You
**My Shining Hour
**One For My Baby (And One More For The Road)

1944

MEET THE PEOPLE (released 1944)
  Heave-Ho, Let The Wind Blow (lyric: E.Y. Harburg)

UP IN ARMS (released March, 1944)
Lyrics by Ted Koehler
 *All Out For Freedom (Dedicated to Anya)
 *Now I Know
 *Tess's Torch Song

KISMET (released August, 1944)
Lyrics by E.Y. Harburg
  *Tell Me, Tell Me, Evening Star
  *Willow In The Wind
BLOOMER GIRL (opened November 5, 1944)
Lyrics by E.Y. Harburg
   Civil War Ballet
  **The Eagle And Me
  **Evelina
   Farmer's Daughter
  *I Got A Song
   I Never Was Born
   It Was Good Enough For Grandma
   Liza Crossing The Ice
   Lullaby (Satin Gown And Silver Shoe)
   Man For Sale
   Pretty As A Picture
   The Rakish Young Man With The Whiskers
 **Right As The Rain
   Simon Legree
   Style Show Ballet
   Sunday In Cicero Falls
  *T'morra, T'morra
   Welcome Hinges
  *When The Boys Come Home
HERE COME THE WAVES (released December, 1944)
Lyrics by Johnny Mercer
 **Ac-cent-tchu-ate The Positive
  *Here Come The Waves
  *I Promise You
 **Let's Take The Long Way Home
   My Mamma Thinks I'm A Star
   The Navy Song
  *There's A Fella Waitin' In Poughkeepsie
   A Woman's Work Is Never Done

1945

OUT OF THIS WORLD (released June, 1945)
Lyrics by Johnny Mercer
  *June Comes Around Every Year
 **Out Of This World

1946

ST. LOUIS WOMAN (opened March 30, 1946)
Lyrics by Johnny Mercer
 **Any Place I Hang My Hat Is Home
  *Cakewalk Your Lady
   Chinquapin Bush
   Come On, Li'l Augie
 **Come Rain Or Come Shine
   High, Low, Jack And The Game
   I Feel My Luck Comin' Down
 **I Had Myself A True Love
 **I Wonder What Became Of Me?
   Least That's My Opinion
   Leavin' Time
  *Legalize My Name
   Li'l Augie Is A Natural Man
   Lim'ricks
***Lullaby
   A Man's Gotta Fight
   Racin' Form
  *Ridin' On The Moon
   Sleep Peaceful, Mr. Used-To-Be
   Somethin' You Gotta Find Out Yourself
   Sow The Seed And Reap The Harvest
   Talkin' Glory
   We Shall Meet To Part, No Never
 **A Woman's Prerogative

1947
*After All (lyric: Ted Koehler)
Got To Wear You Off My Weary Mind (lyric: Johnny Mercer)

1948
CASBAH (released May, 1948)
Lyrics by Leo Robin
**For Every Man There's A Woman
**Hooray For Love
**It Was Written In The Stars
The Monkey Sat In The Cocoanut Tree
**What's Good About Goodbye?

1949
Tell Me In Your Own Sweet Way (lyric: Bob Hilliard)

1950
THE PETTY GIRL (released August, 1950)
Lyrics by Johnny Mercer
*Ah Loves Ya!
*The Calypso Song
*Fancy Free
The Petty Girl
MY BLUE HEAVEN (released September, 1950)
Lyrics by Ralph Blane & Harold Arlen
Cosmo Cosmetics
*Don't Rock The Boat, Dear
*The Friendly Islands
*Halloween
*I Love A New Yorker
*It's Deductible
*Live Hard, Work Hard, Love Hard
What A Man!

1951
MR. IMPERIUM (released October, 1951)
Lyrics by Dorothy Fields
*Andiamo
*Let Me Look At You
*My Love An' My Mule

1953
DOWN AMONG THE SHELTERING PALMS (released June, 1953)
Lyrics by Ralph Blane & Harold Arlen
Back Where I Come From
From Island To Island
I'm A Ruler Of A South Sea Island
Inspection
The Opposite Sex
Twenty-seven Elm Street
What Make De Diff'rence?
When You're In Love
**Who Will It Be When The Time Comes?

THE FARMER TAKES A WIFE (released June, 1953)
Lyrics by Dorothy Fields
Can You Spell Schenectady?
The Erie Canal
I Could Cook
Look Who's Been Dreaming
On The Erie Canal
Somethin' Real Special
**Today I Love Ev'rybody
We're Doin' It For The Natives In Jamaica
We're In Business
When I Close My Door
**With The Sun Warm Upon Me
Yes!

1954
There's No Substitute For A Man (lyric: Howard Dietz)
A STAR IS BORN (released October, 1954)
Lyrics by Ira Gershwin
    Dancing Partner
  *Gotta Have Me Go With You
    Green Light Ahead
  *Here's What I'm Here For
    I'm Off The Downbeat
  *It's A New World
  *Lose That Long Face
 **The Man That Got Away
  *Someone At Last
    The T.V. Commercial
THE COUNTRY GIRL (released December, 1954)
Lyrics by Ira Gershwin
 **Dissertation On The State Of Bliss (Love And Learn)
    It's Mine, It's Yours (The Pitchman)
    The Land Around Us
  *The Search Is Through
HOUSE OF FLOWERS (opened December 30, 1954)
Lyrics by Truman Capote & Harold Arlen
  *Can I Leave Off Wearin' My Shoes?
 **Don't Like Goodbyes
    Has I Let You Down?
 **House Of Flowers
    House Of Flowers Waltz
 **I Never Has Seen Snow
    Indoor Girl (lyric: Michael Brown)
    Love's No Stranger To Me
    Madame Tango's Tango
    Mardi Gras
    Monday Through Sunday
  *One Man (Ain' Quite Enough)
 **A Sleepin' Bee
    Slide, Boy, Slide
  *Smellin' Of Vanilla
    Turtle Song (One Lone Man Against The Sea)
  *Two Ladies In De Shade Of De Banana Tree
  *Waitin'
    What A Man Won't Do For A Woman
  *What Is A Friend For?

1956
Stay Out Of My Dreams (lyric: E.Y. Harburg)

1957
JAMAICA (opened October 31, 1957)
Lyrics by E.Y. Harburg
 **Ain' It De Truth? (note: written for the film CABIN IN THE SKY)
 **Cocoanut Sweet
    For Every Fish (There's A Little Bigger Fish)
    Hooray For De Yankee Dollar
  *I Don't Think I'll End It All Today
    Incompatibility
    Leave De Atom Alone
  *Little Biscuit
    Monkey In The Mango
  *Napoleon
    Pity De Sunset
  *Pretty To Walk With
 **Push De Button
  *Savannah
    Savannah's Wedding Day
  *Take It Slow, Joe
***There's A Sweet Wind Blowin' My Way
    What Did Noah Do (When The Big Wind Came)?
  *What Good Does It Do?
    Whippoorwill

1958
In The Middle Of the Night (lyric: Paddy Chayefsky)

1959
SARATOGA (opened December 7, 1959)
Lyrics by Johnny Mercer
  Al Fresco
  Bon Appetit (Menu Song)
  Countin' Our Chickens
  The Cure
 *Dog Eat Dog
 *A Game Of Poker
**Goose Never Be A Peacock
  Have You Heard? (Gossip Song)
  Here Goes Nothing (note: earlier lyric for "You Or No One")
  I'll Be Respectable
  I'm Headed For Big Things
  Lessons In Love
 *Love Held Lightly
 *The Man In My Life
  One Step, Two Step
 *The Parks Of Paris
 *Petticoat High
  Promenade (Market Cries)
  Reading The News
 *Saratoga
  Workman's Song
 *You For Me
  You Or No One

FREE AND EASY (BLUES OPERA) (opened December 17, 1959)
Lyrics by Johnny Mercer
  A Baby's Born; Bees 'n' Flowers; Bettin' Calls; Black Magic; Blind Man; Blow De Whistle; Blues; Blues In The Night; Boogie; Cake Song; Cakewalk Turns; Soft-Shoe; Sword Dance; Cakewalk Your Lady; Champagne Fo' De Lady; Come Rain Or Come Shine; Conjure Man; Curse; De Right Answer; Della's Entrance (Watcha Sayin' Della?); Dis Is De Day; Dis Little While; Dissolves; Dixieland; Dressing Up Sequence; (Ridin' On The Moon); Easy Street; Elegy; First March; Fix Yo'self Up; Flower Vendor; Free And Easy (Any Place I Hang My Hat Is Home); Genteel Bastard; High Low, Jack And The Game; Higher Den De Moon; I Ain't Afraid; I Gotta Right To Sing The Blues; I Had Myself A True Love; I Wonder What Became Of Me; Ill Wind; Killing Sequence; Ladies 'n' Gentlemen; Least That's My Opinion; Leavin' Time; Legalize My Name; Like Clouds Up In The Sky; Live Hard, Work Hard, Love Hard; Look What A Hole You're In; Lookin' Fo' Somebody; Lullaby; Lumpin'; Many Kinds Of Love; Minuet; Natchul Man; News Chant; One For The Road; Pandemonium; Race; Racin' Forms; Rainbow; Reap The Harvest; Second March; Second Wind; Sleep Peaceful, Mr. Used-To-Be; Snake Eyes; Somethin' Ya Gotta Find Out Yo'self; Streak O' Lightnin'; Sweetnin' Water; Tambourine; Tangissimo; Then Suddenly; Third March; Toastin' Sequence; Waltz, Dixieland; Whatcha Sayin'?; Wheel 'Em and Deal 'Em; A Woman's Prerogative; Won't Dat Be De Blessed Day?; Ya Pushin' Ya Luck

1960
 *Ode (for solo piano)
  Bon-Bon (for solo piano)

1961
**Happy With The Blues (lyric: Peggy Lee)

1962
Abstractions (The Flight Of The Sleeping Pill) for solo piano
**The Morning After (lyric: Dory Langdon)

GAY PURR-EE (released October, 1962)
Lyrics by E.Y. Harburg
  Bubbles
  Free At Last
  The Horse Won't Talk
 **Little Drops Of Rain
  *Mewsette
***The Money Cat
 **Paris Is A Lonely Town
  *Roses Red - Violets Blue
  Take My Hand Paree

1963
**So Long, Big Time! (lyric: Dory Langdon)
 *You're Impossible (lyric: Dory Langdon)
  Bad For Each Other (lyric: Carolyn Leigh)
***The Silent Spring (lyric: E.Y. Harburg)

I COULD GO ON SINGING (released March, 1963)
 *I Could Go On Singing (Till The Cows Come Home) (lyric: E.Y. Harburg)

1964
Hurt But Happy (lyric: Dory Langdon)
I Could Be Good For You (lyric: Martin Charnin)

1965
**That's A Fine Kind O' Freedom (lyric: Martin Charnin)
A Girl's Entitled (lyric: Martin Charnin)
John - John - John (John V. Lindsay) (lyric: Martin Charnin)
Let's Give The Job To Lindsay (lyric: Martin Charnin)
Little Travelbug (lyric: Martin Charnin)
Shoulda Stood In Bed (lyric: Martin Charnin)
Summer In Brooklyn (lyric: Martin Charnin)
This Ol' World (lyric: Martin Charnin)

1966
Come On, Midnight (lyric: Martin Charnin)
Spring Has Me Out On A Limb (lyric: Martin Charnin) (note: lyric incomplete)
SOFTLY (unproduced musical)
Lyrics by Martin Charnin
  Baby San
  Been A Hell Of An Evening
  The Brush Off
  Don't Say "Love" - I've Been There And Back
  Fish Go Higher Than Tigers
  Happy Any Day
  Hello (Herro)
  I Will
  Momma Knows Best
  The More You See Of It
  My Lady Fair
  Once I Wore Ribbons Here
  Suddenly The Sunrise
  Temples
  We Were Always To Be Married
  Works Both Ways
  Why Do You Make Me Like You?
  Yellow Rain
  You Are Tomorrow
  You're Never Fully Dressed Without A Smile

1968

HOUSE OF FLOWERS (revival) (opened January 28, 1968)
Lyrics by Truman Capote & Harold Arlen
   Albertina's Beautiful Hair
   Dark Song
   Do Not Be Afraid Of Love
  *Jump De Broom
  *Madame Tango's Particular Tango
  *Somethin' Cold To Drink
   Walk To De Grave
  *Wife Never Understan'
   The Wonders Of A Barrel

1970

   Runaway World (lyric: Bud McCreery) (note: lyric version of Ode)

1973

CLIPPETY CLOP AND CLEMENTINE (unproduced musical for television)
Lyrics by Harold Arlen
   Clippety Clop And Clementine
   Dreamin' Suits Me Just Fine
   A Happy Recipe (A Nonsense Song)
***I Had A Love Once
   Is What It's All About
   Organic Food
   Ridin' Through The Park In A Hansom Cab
   This Way Or No Way At All

1976

   Looks Like The End Of A Beautiful Friendship (lyric: E.Y. Harburg)
***Promise Me Not To Love Me (lyric: E.Y. Harburg)

Harold Arlen at the piano with his dog, Shmutts

E.Y. Harburg and Harold Arlen at the time of THE WIZARD OF OZ

E.Y. Harburg & Harold Arlen 40 years after
THE WIZARD OF OZ

Ted Koehler and Harold Arlen

Harold Arlen with Ira Gershwin on the tennis court

Harold Arlen with Marlene Dietrich and Noel Coward

Harold Arlen working on the score of GAY PURR-EE

GET HAPPY
(From The Musical Production "Nine-Fifteen Revue")

Lyric by TED KOEHLER
Music by HAROLD ARLEN

26

sins 'way in the tide. It's all so peace-ful on the oth-er

side____ For-get your troub-les and just GET HAP-PY____ You bet-ter

chase all your cares a-way____ Shout Hal-le-lu-jah! come on, GET

HAP-PY____ Get read-y for the judge-ment day For-get your day____

BETWEEN THE DEVIL AND THE DEEP BLUE SEA

(From The Musical Production "Rhythmania")

Lyric by TED KOEHLER
Music by HAROLD ARLEN

de-vil and the deep blue sea, ___ I ought to cross you off my list, ___ but when you come knocking

at my door, ___ Fate seems to give my heart a twist, and I come run-ning back for

more, I should hate you, but I guess I love you,

You've got me in be-tween ___ the de-vil and the deep blue sea. ___

I GOTTA RIGHT TO SING THE BLUES

(From The Musical Production "Earl Carroll's Vanities")

Lyric by TED KOEHLER
Music by HAROLD ARLEN

right to sit and cry __ down a - round the riv - er. I know the

deep blue sea __ Will soon be call-ing me. __

It must be love say what you choose, I got-ta right to sing the blues. __

I got - ta

SATAN'S LI'L LAMB
(From The Musical Production "Americana")

Lyric by E.Y. HARBURG & JOHNNY MERCER
Music by HAROLD ARLEN

*Symbols for Guitar and Banjo

I'VE GOT THE WORLD ON A STRING

(From "Cotton Club Parade - 21st Edition")

Tune Ukulele
G C E A

Lyric by TED KOEHLER
Music by HAROLD ARLEN

CHORUS

I've got the world on a string, ___ sit-tin' on a rain-bow, Got the string a-round my fin-

___ ger, What a world, what a life, ___ I'm in love! I've got a

song that I sing, ___ I can make the rain go, an-y time I move my fin - - ger,

Luck-y me, can't you see, I'm in love, ___ Life is a beau-ti-ful thing, ___

40

as long as I hold the string,___ I'd be a sil-ly so-and-so,

if I should ev-er let go,_____ I've got the world on a string,___

sit-tin' on a rain-bow, Got the string a-round my fin - ger, What a world, what a_

___ life, I'm in love!_____ I've got the love._____ Bell

THE WAIL OF THE REEFER MAN
(From "Cotton Club Parade - 21st Edition)

Tune Ukulele

A D F# B

Capo on 1st fret

Lyric by TED KOEHLER
Music by HAROLD ARLEN

When day is done and a veil night has spun soft-ly blan-kets a tired wea-ry world, Then the Reef-er

Man reach-es those he can with his mourn-ful plan._____

CHORUS

Hap-pi-ness for sale, Hap-pi-ness for sale, Dreams who'll buy them, Dreams who'll try them?

Buy my wares, drown your cares, That's the wail of the Reef-er Man,

When your woes sur-round you, don't let trou-ble hound you, Dreams may tum-ble, let them crumble,

Joy is near when you hear the wail of the Reef-er Man

43

Soon as the night starts ____ de-scend-ing, and brok-en-down hearts ____ need mend-ing,____

His wear-y way he _____ starts wend-ing, wail - in' thru the night,

Hap-pi-ness for sale, Hap-pi-ness for sale, Dreams who'll buy them, Dreams who'll try them? Buy my wares,

1.

2.

drown your cares, That's the wail of the Reef-er Man. Man.____

IT'S ONLY A PAPER MOON
(From The Musical Production "The Great Magoo")

Lyric by BILLY ROSE and E.Y. HARBURG
Music by HAROLD ARLEN

mm, A bub-ble for a min-ute, Mm,

mm, You smile, the bub-ble has a rain-bow in it.

Say, it's on-ly a pa-per moon, Sail-ing o-ver a

card-board sea, But it would-n't be make be-lieve, If you_

46

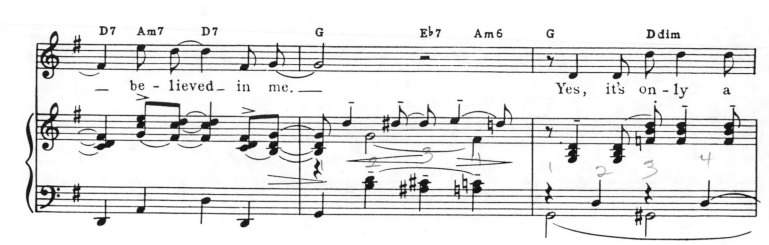

-rade, With - out your love, it's a

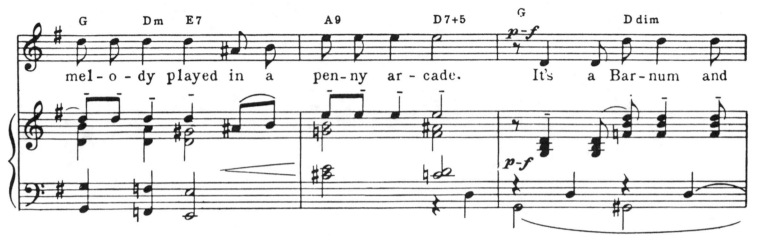

mel - o - dy played in a pen-ny ar - cade. It's a Bar-num and

Bai-ley world,— Just as phon-y as it can be,— But it would-n't be

make be - lieve If you— be-lieved— in me.—

STORMY WEATHER
(Keeps Rainin' All The Time)
(From "Cotton Club Parade - 22nd Edition")

Lyric by TED KOEHLER
Music by HAROLD ARLEN

LET'S FALL IN LOVE
(From The Motion Picture "Let's Fall In Love")

Lyric by TED KOEHLER
Music by HAROLD ARLEN

HAPPY AS THE DAY IS LONG
(From "Cotton Club Parade - 22nd Edition")

Lyric by TED KOEHLER
Music by HAROLD ARLEN

like a' mil-lion-aire,'cause I'm hap-py as the day is long,__ Got a heav-y af-fair,__ and__ I'm

hav-in' my fun,__ Am I walk-in' on air?__ Gee, but I'm the luck-y one!__ I've got my

peace of mind,__Knock wood,"I hear that love is blind,__ that's good,'Cause the things I nev-er see nev-er

seem to wor-ry me, So I'm hap-py as the day is long._____ I've got my   long.

ILL WIND

(You're Blowin' Me No Good)

(From "Cotton Club Parade - 24th Edition")

Lyric by TED KOEHLER
Music by HAROLD ARLEN

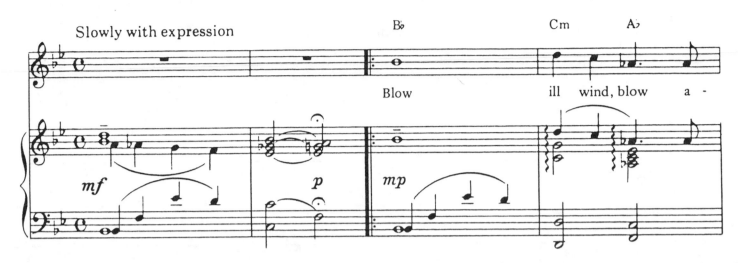

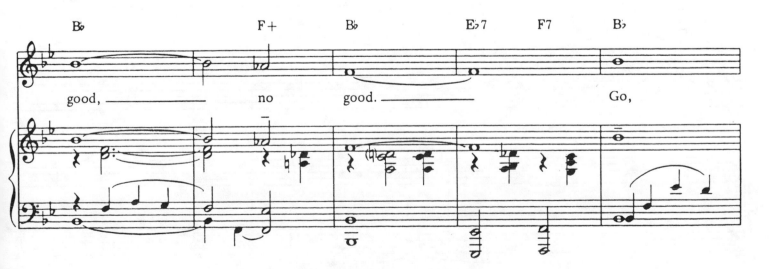

ill wind, go a-way, Skies are, oh, so gray _____ A-

round my neigh-bor-hood, _____ and that's no good. _____

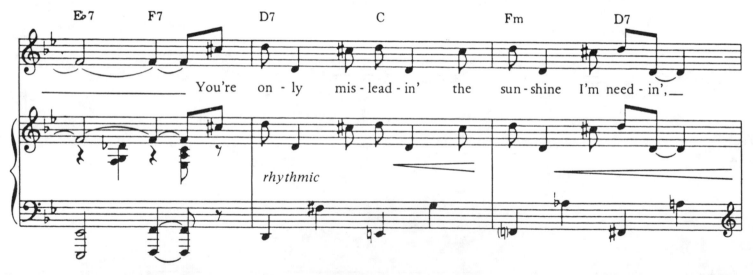

_____ You're on-ly mis-lead-in' the sun-shine I'm need-in', _____

rhythmic

Ain't that a shame? _____ It's so hard to keep up with

FUN TO BE FOOLED
(From The Musical Production "Life Begins At 8:40")

Lyric by IRA GERSHWIN and E.Y. HARBURG
Music by HAROLD ARLEN

Symbols for Ukulele, Tenor-Guitar and Banjo

Thought I was done,___ Still, it is fun___ Be-ing fooled a -

gain.___ Nice when you tell___ All that you feel,___

Nice to be told ___ This is the real thing;

Fun to be kissed,___ Fun to ex - ist,___ To be fooled a - gain.___

AS LONG AS I LIVE

(From "Cotton Club Parade - 24th Edition")

Lyric by TED KOEHLER
Music by HAROLD ARLEN

CHORUS

May-be I can't live to love_ you as long as I want to, Life is-n't long e-nough,

ba - by, But I can love you as long as I live.

May-be I can't give you dia - monds and things like I want to, But I can prom-ise you,

ba - by, I'm gon-na want to as long as I live. I nev-er cared, but I'll ev-en wear long

LET'S TAKE A WALK AROUND THE BLOCK

(From The Musical Production "Life Begins At 8:40")

Lyric by IRA GERSHWIN and E.Y. HARBURG
Music by HAROLD ARLEN

I nev-er tra-vel'd fur-ther north than old Van Cort-landt Park,___ And

nev-er fur-ther south than the A-qua-ri-um;___ I've

seen the charm of Jer-sey Ci-ty But, first let me re-mark,___ I

Symbols for Ukulele,
Tenor-Guitar and Banjo

LAST NIGHT WHEN WE WERE YOUNG

Lyric by E.Y. HARBURG
Music by HAROLD ARLEN

*) *Symbols for Guitar, Chords for Ukulele and Banjo*

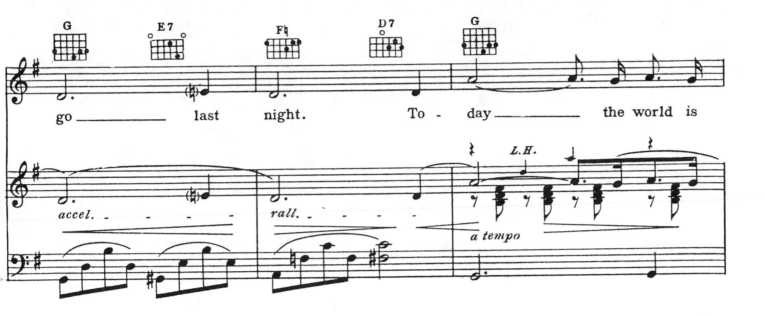

go _____ last night. To - day _____ the world is

accel. _ _ _ _ *rall.* _ _ _ _ *a tempo*

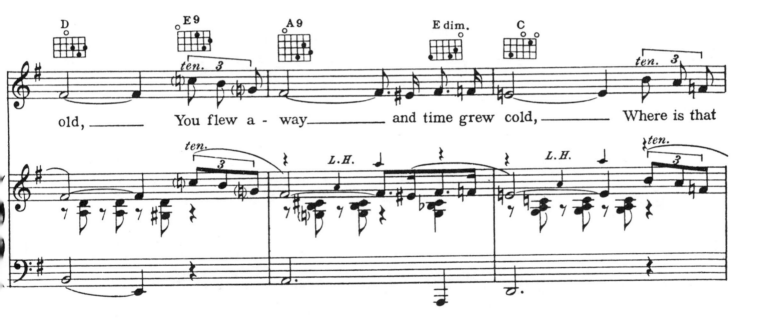

old, _____ You flew a - way _____ and time grew cold, _____ Where is that

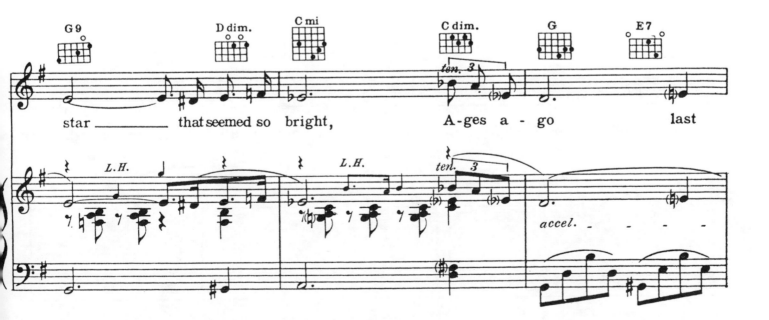

star _____ that seemed so bright, A - ges a - go last

accel. _ _ _ _

night? To think _____ that spring had de - pend - ed _____ on mere-ly

this _____ a look, a kiss. To think _____ that some-thing so

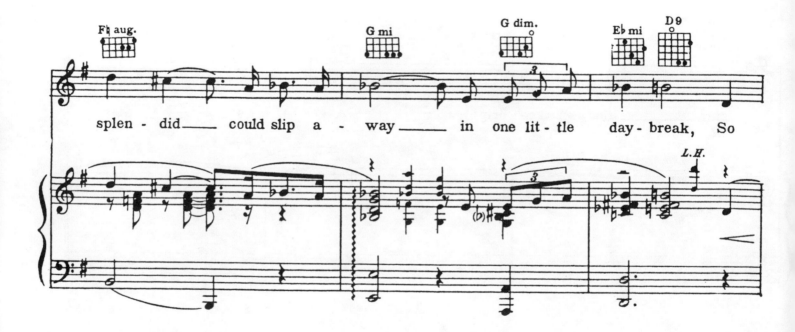

splen - did____ could slip a - way ____ in one lit - tle day - break, So

YOU'RE THE CURE FOR WHAT AILS ME
(From The Motion Picture "The Singing Kid")

Lyric by E.Y. HARBURG
Music by HAROLD ARLEN

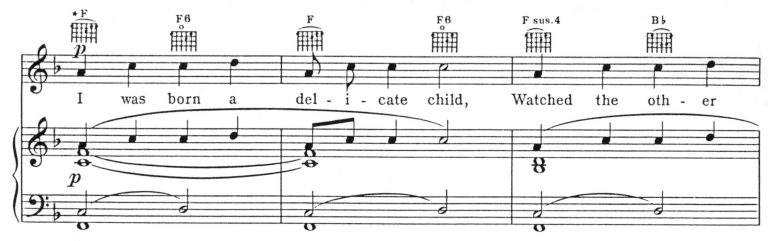

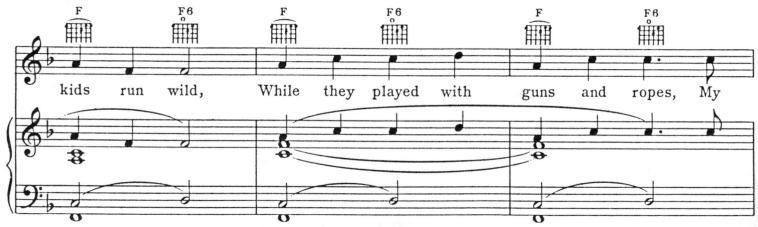

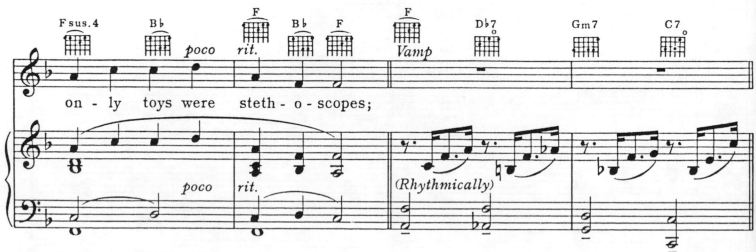

*Symbols are for Ukulele, Banjo and Guitar

REFRAIN

I was a chron-ic___ "How've yuh been?"___ Then like a ton-ic___

you blew in,___ You're the cure for what ails me___ and you do___ me good,

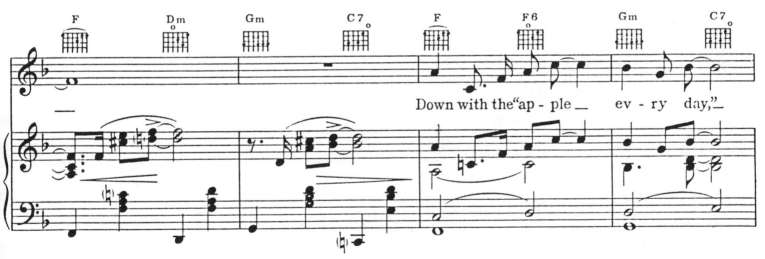

Down with the "ap - ple___ ev - ry day,"

Down with the ul - tra___ vio - let ray,___ You're the cure for what ails me___

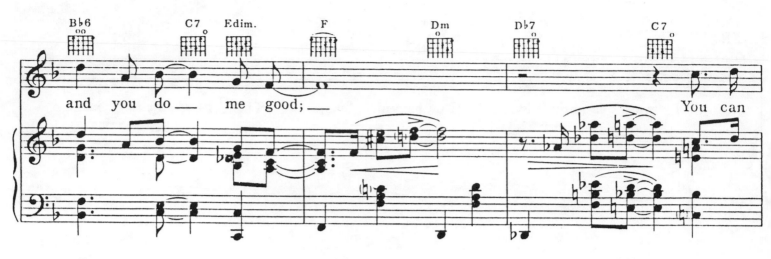

and you do ___ me good; ___ You can

go starve a fe-ver, you can feed a cold, _ But I don't fear fe-ver and I

can't catch cold, you're my pink _____ of con - dish' _____ You're my

Ar - row-head Springs, and my Bat - tle Creek, Mich. I was a meek-ie, ___

FANCY MEETING YOU

(From The Motion Picture "Stage Struck")

Lyric by E.Y. HARBURG
Music by HAROLD ARLEN

*Symbols for Ukulele, Guitar and Banjo

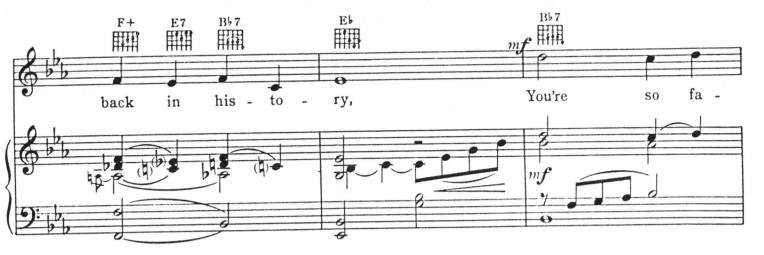

back in his - to - ry, You're so fa -

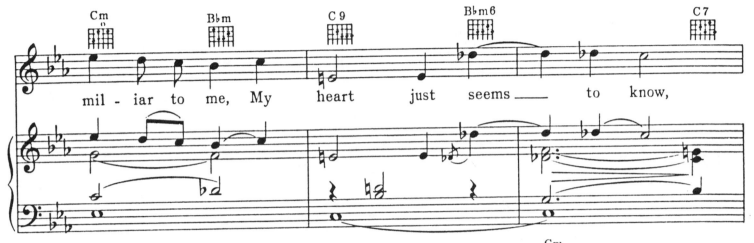

mil - iar to me, My heart just seems ___ to know,

We've been brought to - geth - er a - gain, Out of the long a -

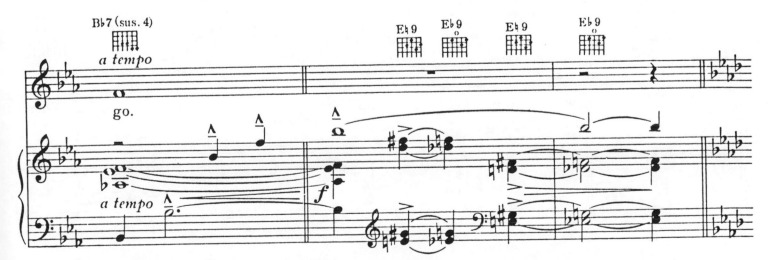

go.

WHEN THE WIND BLOWS SOUTH

Lyric by E.Y. HARBURG
Music by HAROLD ARLEN

GOD'S COUNTRY
(From The Musical Production "Hooray For What!")

Lyric by E.Y. HARBURG
Music by HAROLD ARLEN

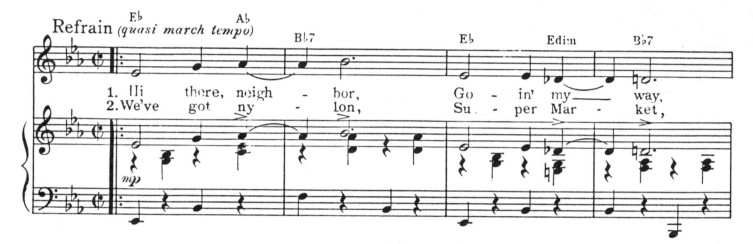

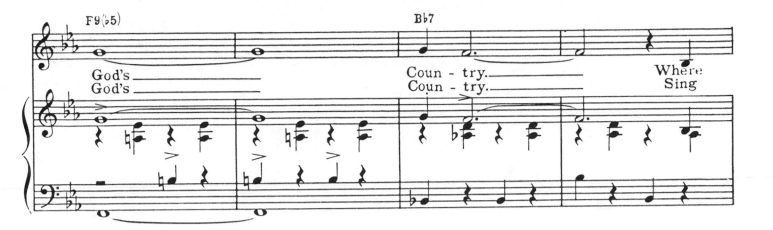

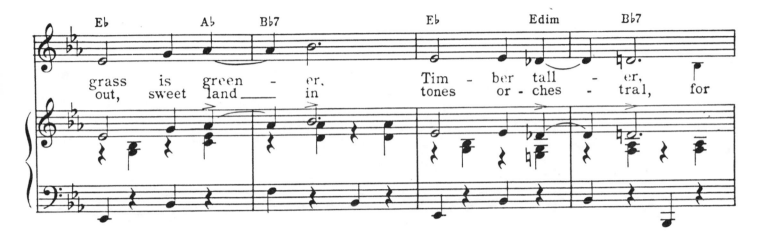

90

God's _____ Coun - try. A hun-dred mil - lion
God's _____ Coun - try. Ten mil - lion rock 'n

root-ers can't be wrong, So give a hand, give a hand, Give a cheer for the
roll-ers can't be wrong, So give a yell, give a yell, Give a shout, all is

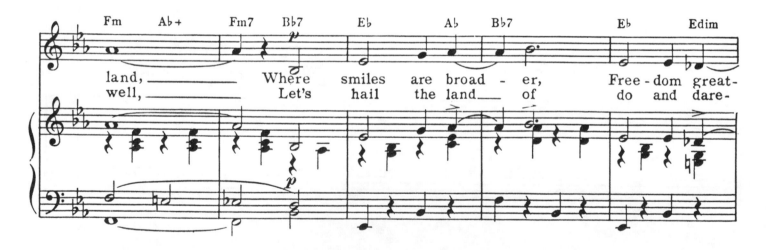

land, _____ Where smiles are broad - er, Free - dom great-
well, _____ Let's hail the land ___ of do and dare-

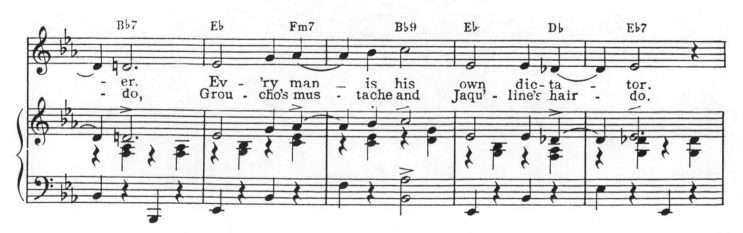

- er. Ev - 'ry man ___ is his own dic - ta - tor.
- do, Grou - cho's mus - tache and Jaqu' - line's hair - do.

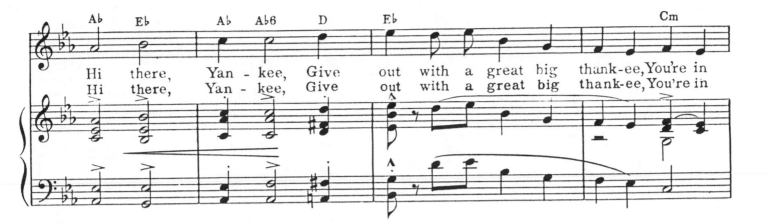

Hi there, Yan-kee, Give out with a great big thank-ee, You're in
Hi there, Yan-kee, Give out with a great big thank-ee, You're in

God's, _____ God's _____
God's, _____ God's _____

1.

Coun - try! _____

2.

Coun - try!

sf

MOANIN' IN THE MORNIN'

(From The Musical Production "Hooray For What!")

Lyric by E.Y. HARBURG
Music by HAROLD ARLEN

* Names of chords for Ukulele and Banjo.
Symbols for Guitar.

IN THE SHADE OF THE NEW APPLE TREE
(From The Musical Production "Hooray For What!")

Lyric by E.Y. HARBURG
Music by HAROLD ARLEN

*Names of chords for Ukulele and Banjo.
Symbols for Guitar.

knee, _____ Though the world is new and fan-cy

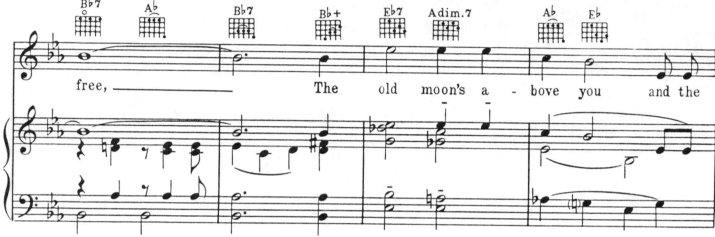

free, _____ The old moon's a - bove you and the

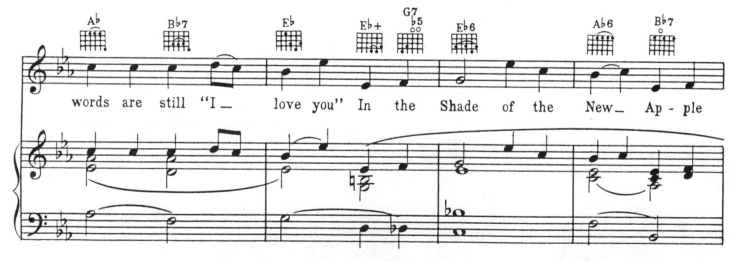

words are still "I _ love you" In the Shade of the New _ Ap - ple

Tree. _____ Gone are all the bon-nets and bows, That

BUDS WON'T BUD
(From The Musical Production "Hooray For What!")

Lyric by E.Y. HARBURG
Music by HAROLD ARLEN

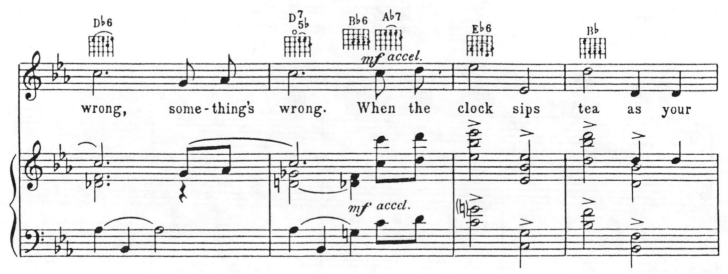

tears won't dry;— And— to make— things worse, My
mind won't mind;— And— it all — seems like,— The

heart is beat-ing in re-verse,— 'Cause— buds won't bud, breeze won't breeze And
world is on a sit-down strike,— 'Cause— buds won't bud, breeze won't breeze And

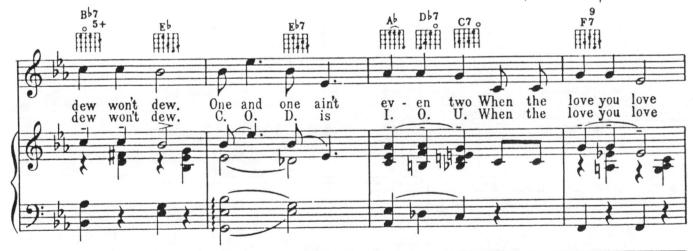

dew won't dew. One and one ain't ev-en two When the love you love
dew won't dew. C. O. D. is I. O. U. When the love you love

won't love you.

won't come through. _____

DOWN WITH LOVE

(From The Musical Production "Hooray For What!")

Lyric by E.Y. HARBURG
Music by HAROLD ARLEN

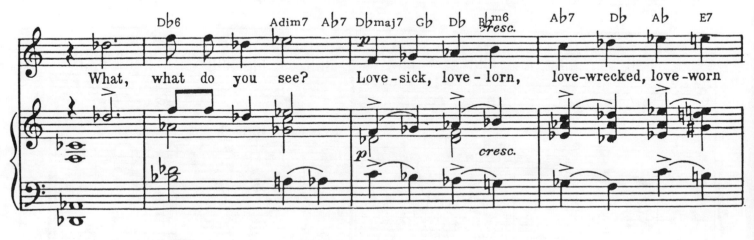

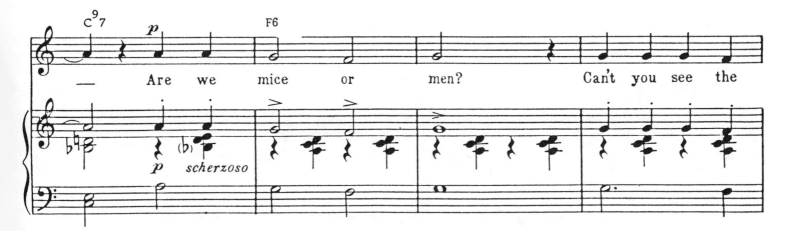

way. _____ Give it back to the birds and the bees and the Vi- en-

nese, _____ Down with eyes ro-man-tic and stu-pid.

Down with sighs, Down with Cu- pid. Broth-er, let's stuff that Dove. Down with

love! _____   love! _____

WHEN THE SUN COMES OUT

Lyric by TED KOEHLER
Music by HAROLD ARLEN

OVER THE RAINBOW

(From The Motion Picture "The Wizard Of Oz")

Lyric by E.Y. HARBURG
Music by HAROLD ARLEN

Chorus, Moderately (*Not fast*)

Some - where O - ver The Rain-bow skies are blue, And the

dreams that you dare to dream real-ly do come true. Some-day I'll wish up-on a star and

wake up where the clouds are far be-hind me,___ Where troub-les melt like lem-on drops, a-

-way, a - bove the chim-ney tops that's where you'll find me. Some - where

DING-DONG! THE WITCH IS DEAD

(From The Motion Picture "The Wizard Of Oz")

Lyric by E.Y. HARBURG
Music by HAROLD ARLEN

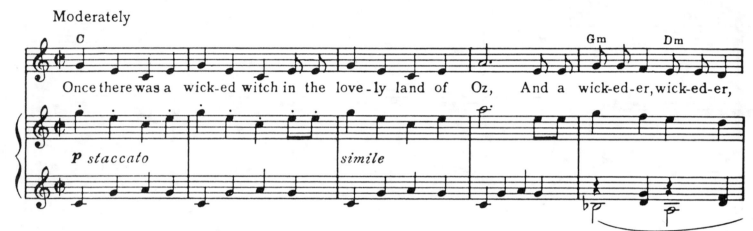

Once there was a wick-ed witch in the love-ly land of Oz, And a wick-ed-er, wick-ed-er,

wick-ed-er witch there nev-er, nev-er was. She filled the folks in Munch-kin land with

ter-ror and with dread, 'Till one fine day from Kan-sas way a cy-clone caught a

house that brought the wick-ed, wick-ed witch her doom as she was fly-ing on her broom_

For the house fell on her head and the cor-o-ner pro-

-nounced her dead,_____ And

thru the town the joy-ous news was spread._____

Chorus, Moderately

Ding - Dong, The Witch Is Dead! Which old witch? the wick-ed witch.

Ding - dong, the wick-ed witch is dead._____ Wake up, you

sleep - y head, rub your eyes, get out of bed. Wake up, the

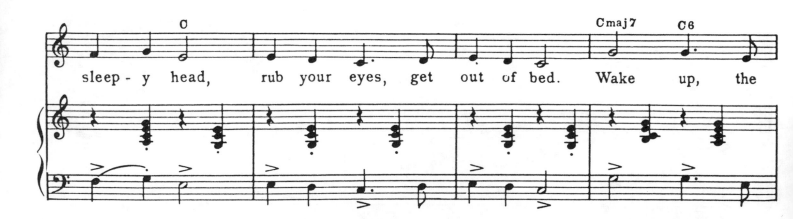

wick - ed witch is dead!_____ She's gone where the gob-lins go be-

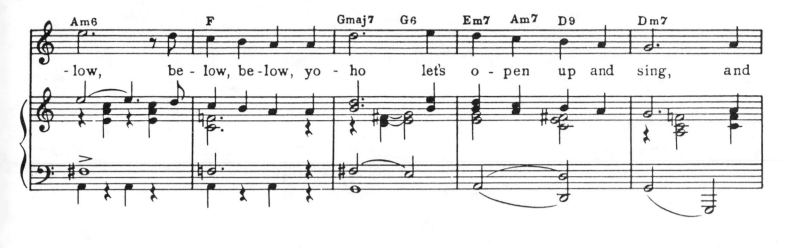

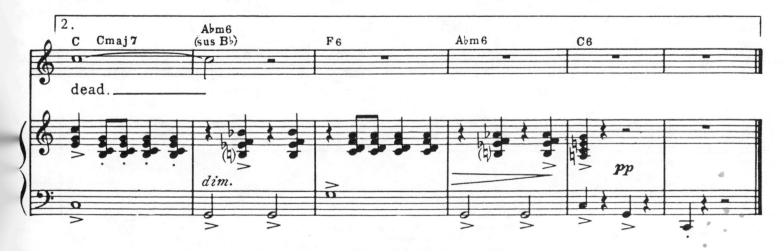

IF I ONLY HAD A BRAIN
(From The Motion Picture "The Wizard Of Oz")

Lyric by E.Y. HARBURG
Music by HAROLD ARLEN

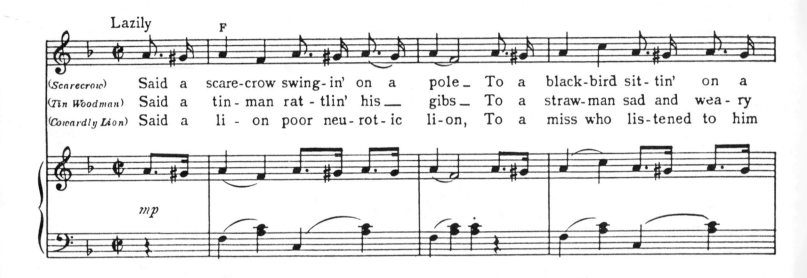

(Scarecrow) Said a scare-crow swing-in' on a pole___ To a black-bird sit-tin' on a
(Tin Woodman) Said a tin-man rat-tlin' his___ gibs___ To a straw-man sad and wea-ry
(Cowardly Lion) Said a li-on poor neu-rot-ic li-on, To a miss who lis-tened to him

fence___ "Oh! the Lord gave me a soul___ But for-
eyed,___ "Oh! the Lord gave me tin ribs___ But for-
rave,___ "Oh! the Lord made me a li-on, But the

-got to give me com-mon sense.___ If I had an ounce of com-mon sense."
-got to put a heart in - side." Then he banged his hol - low chest and cried.
Lord for-got to make me brave." Then his tail be-gan to curl and wave.

Chorus, Moderately

(Scarecrow) I could while a-way the hours___ con - ferr - in' with the flow'rs con-
(Tin Woodman) When a man's an emp - ty ket-tle he should be on his met-tle and
(Cowardly Lion) Life is sad be-lieve me mis-sy when you're born to be a sis-sy, with-

-sult - in' with the rain___ And my head, I'd be scratch-in' while my
yet I'm torn a part___ Just be-cause I'm pre-sum - in' that I
-out the vim and verve___ But I could change my hab - its, nev - er

thoughts were bus - y hatch - in' If I On - ly Had A Brain.___ I'd un-
could be kind - a hu - man If I On - ly Had A Heart.___ I'd be
more be scared of rab - bits If I On - ly Had The Nerve.___ I'm a-

122

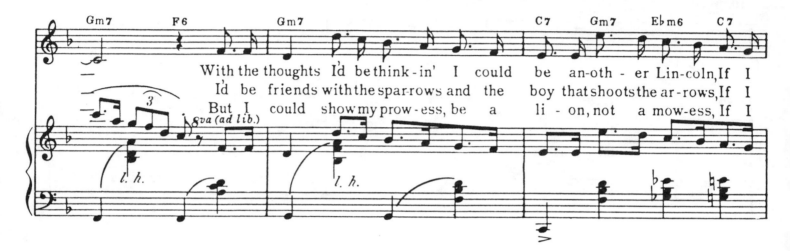

-rav-el ev-'ry rid-dle   for an-y in-di-vid-le   in troub-le or in pain___
ten-der, I'd be gen-tle   and aw-ful sen-ti-men-tal   re-gard-ing love and art___
-fraid there's no de-ny-in'   I'm just a dan-dy-li-on,   A fate I don't de-serve___

With the thoughts I'd be think-in' I could   be an-oth-er Lin-coln, If I
I'd be friends with the spar-rows and the   boy that shoots the ar-rows, If I
But I could show my prow-ess, be a   li-on, not a mow-ess, If I

On-ly Had A Brain.___   Oh, I___ could tell you why   the
On-ly Had A Heart.___   Pic-ture me___ a bal-co-ny   a-
On-ly Had The Nerve.___   Oh, I'd___ be in my stride,   a

o-cean's near the   shore,   I could think of things I   nev-er thunk be-
-bove a voice sings   low,   "Where-fore art   thou, Ro - me -
king down to the   core,   Oh, I'd roar the way I   nev-er roared be-

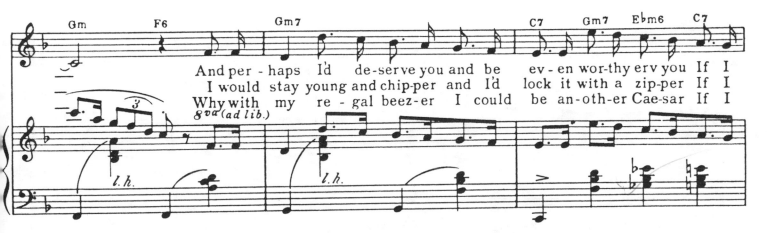

BLUES IN THE NIGHT
(My Mama Done Tol' Me)
(From The Motion Picture "Blues In The Night")

Lyric by JOHNNY MERCER
Music by HAROLD ARLEN

Take my word, the mock - in' bird - 'll sing the

sad - dest kind o' song, he knows things are wrong____ and he's right.____

(whistle)____

From Nat-chez to Mo - bile,__ from Mem-phis to St. Joe,__ wher -

ev - er the four winds— blow;_____ I been in some big towns— an'

heard me some big talk, ___ but there is one thing I know,_____ {A {A

wom - an's a two - face,___ } A wor - ri - some thing who'll leave ya t' sing the
man is a two - face,___ }

Blues_____ In The Night. Hum_____

My ma - ma was right, there's Blues_____ In The Night.

THIS TIME THE DREAM'S ON ME
(From The Motion Picture "Blues In The Night")

Lyric by JOHNNY MERCER
Music by HAROLD ARLEN

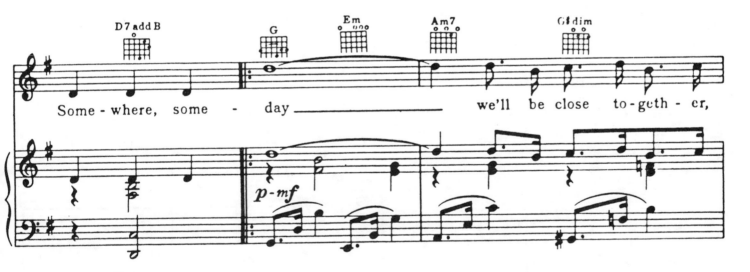

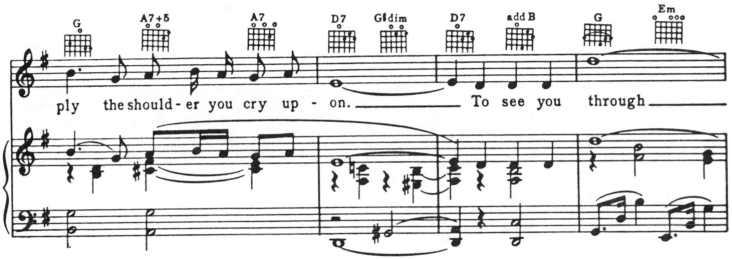

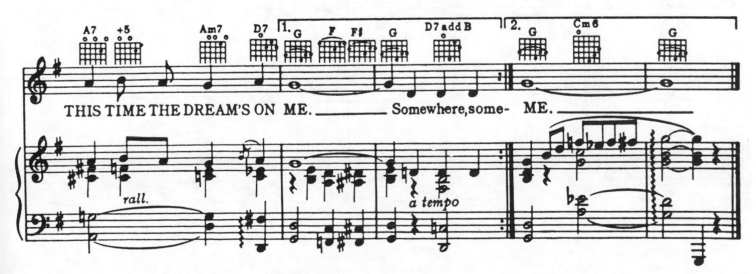

THAT OLD BLACK MAGIC
(From The Motion Picture "Star Spangled Rhythm")

Lyric by JOHNNY MERCER
Music by HAROLD ARLEN

i - cy fin - gers up and down my spine.___ The

same old witch - craft when your eyes meet mine.___ The

same old tin - gle that I feel in - side___ And

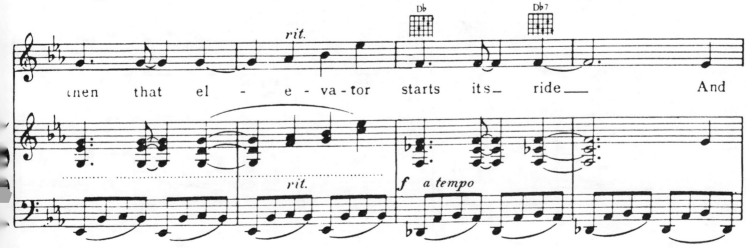

then that el - e - va - tor starts its___ ride___ And

HIT THE ROAD TO DREAMLAND
(From The Motion Picture "Star Spangled Rhythm")

Lyric by JOHNNY MERCER
Music by HAROLD ARLEN

*Chord Names For Guitar

LIFE'S FULL OF CONSEQUENCE

(From The Motion Picture "Cabin In The Sky")

Lyric by E.Y. HARBURG
Music by HAROLD ARLEN

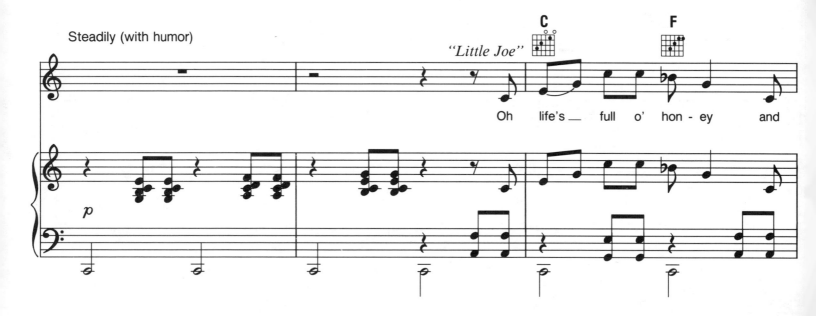

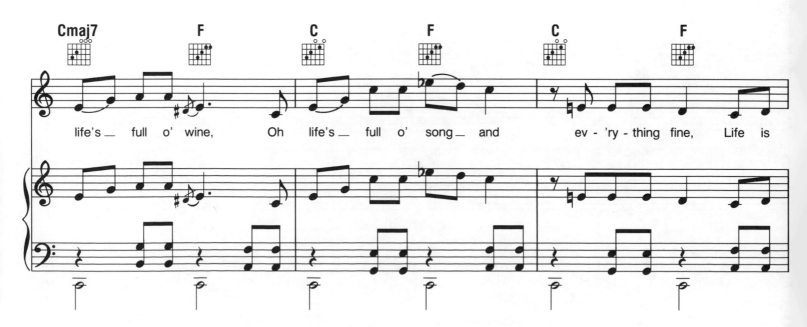

HAPPINESS IS A THING CALLED JOE

(From The Motion Picture "Cabin In The Sky")

Lyric by E.Y. HARBURG
Music by HAROLD ARLEN

AIN' IT DE TRUTH?

(From The Musical Production "Jamaica")

Lyric by E.Y. HARBURG
Music by HAROLD ARLEN

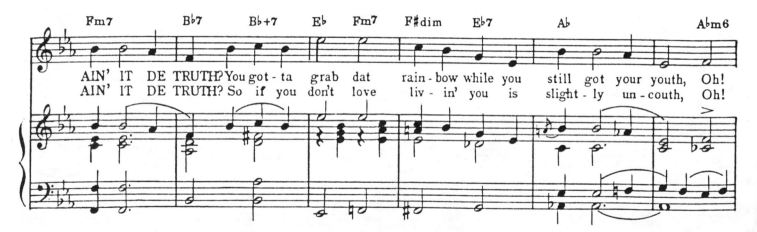

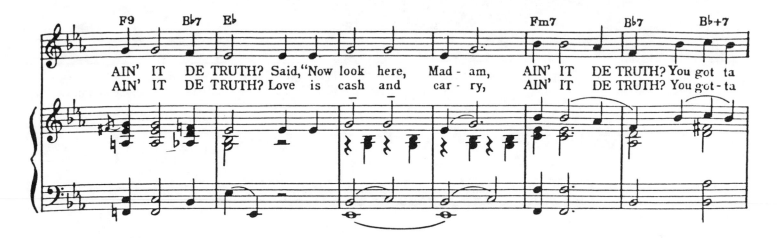

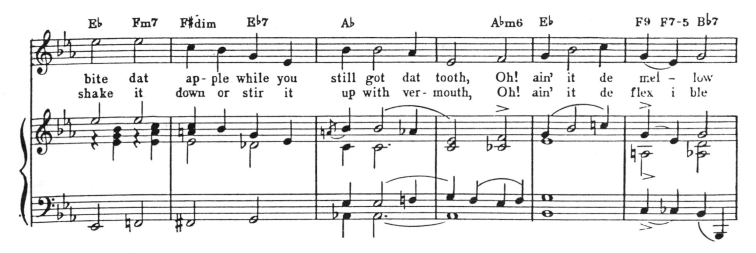

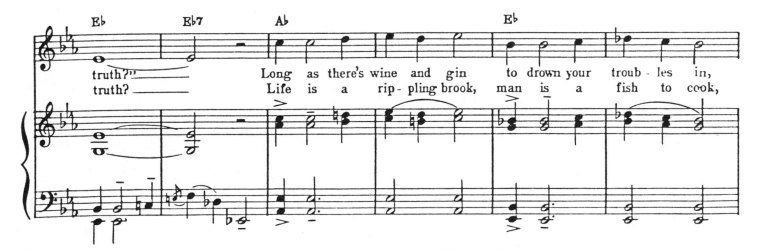

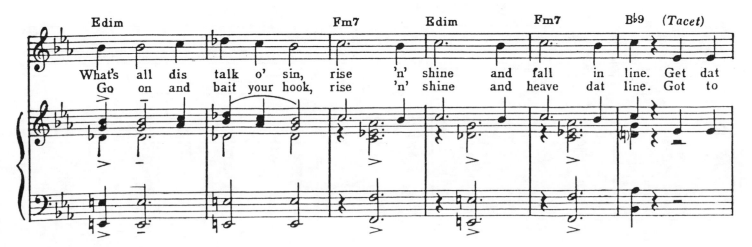

new re - li - gion, AIN' IT DE TRUTH? Fo' you is dead pi - geon,
get your pos - sum, AIN' IT DE TRUTH? While you's still in blos - som,

AIN' IT DE TRUTH? 'Cause when you're laid hor - i - zon - tal in dat tel - e - phone booth,_
AIN' IT DE TRUTH? And dat went for De - li - lah, Cle - o - pat - ra and Ruth,_

Dere'll be no breath - in' spell, dat's on - ly nat - u - ral Ain' it the gos - sip - el
Them babes did might - y swell, they rang that Jez - e - bel, Ain' it the gos - sip - el

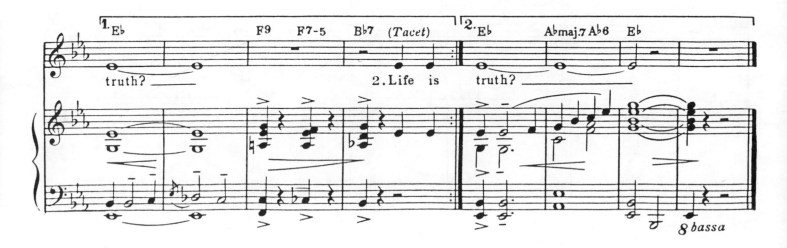

truth?_   2. Life is   truth?_

LIKE A STRAW IN THE WIND

Lyric by TED KOEHLER
Music by HAROLD ARLEN

*Symbols for Guitar, Diagrams for Ukulele.

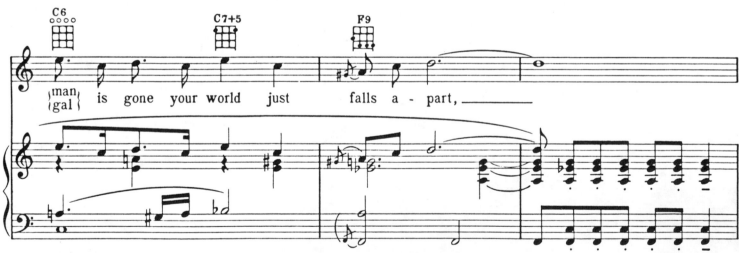

Don't a heart get all the breaks, _____ When your hopes come un-

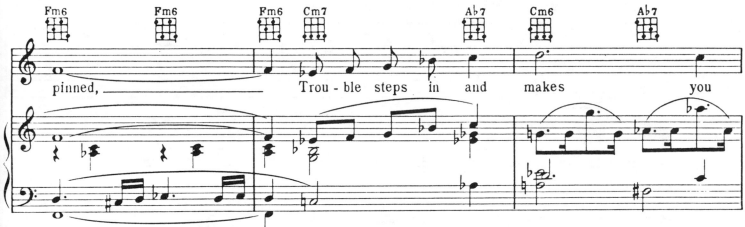

pinned, _____ Trou-ble steps in and makes you

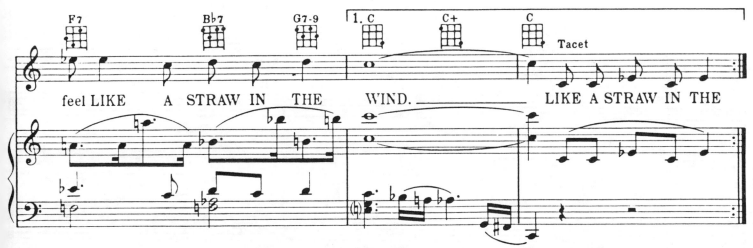

feel LIKE A STRAW IN THE WIND. _____ LIKE A STRAW IN THE

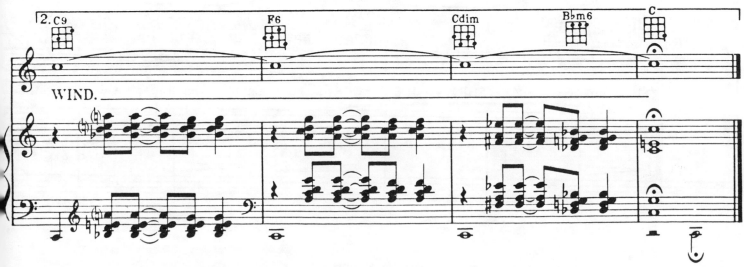

WIND. _____

MY SHINING HOUR
(From The Motion Picture "The Sky's The Limit")

Lyric by JOHNNY MERCER
Music by HAROLD ARLEN

ONE FOR MY BABY
(And One More For The Road)
(From The Motion Picture "The Sky's The Limit")

Lyric by JOHNNY MERCER
Music by HAROLD ARLEN

Lazily

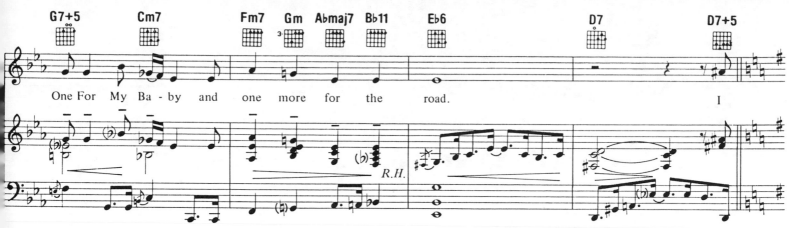

One For My Ba - by and one more for the road. I

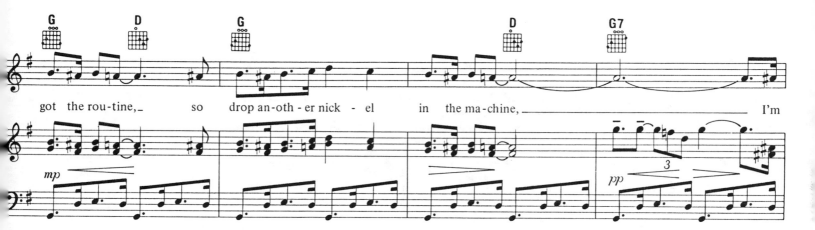

got the rou-tine,_ so drop an-oth-er nick - el in the ma-chine, _____ I'm

feel - in' so bad,_ I wish you'd make the mu - sic dream-y and sad, _____ Could

tell you a lot,_ But you've got_ to be true to your code, _____ Make it

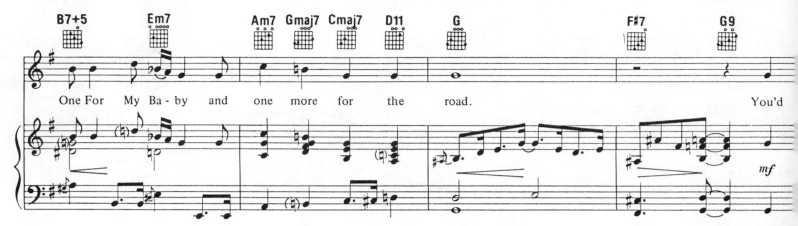

One For My Ba-by and one more for the road. You'd

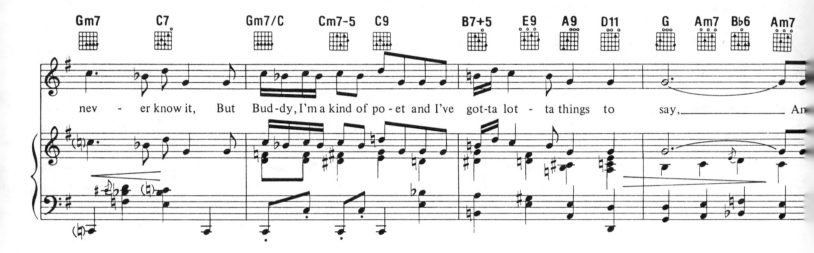

nev - er know it, But Bud-dy, I'm a kind of po - et and I've got-ta lot - ta things to say,_____ An

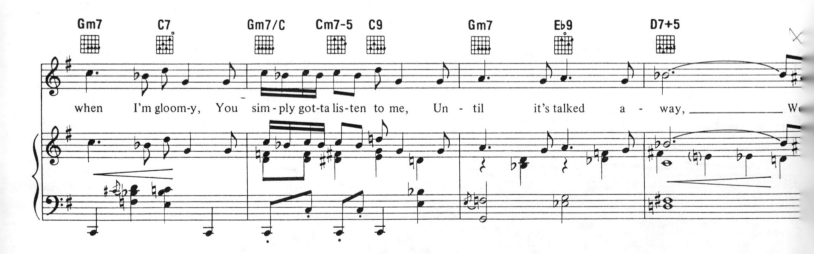

when I'm gloom-y, You sim - ply got-ta lis-ten to me, Un - til it's talked a - way,_____ We

that's how it goes___ And Joe, I know you're get - ting anx - ious to close,_____ An

thanks for the cheer,___ I hope you did-n't mind my bend-ing your ear,_____ This

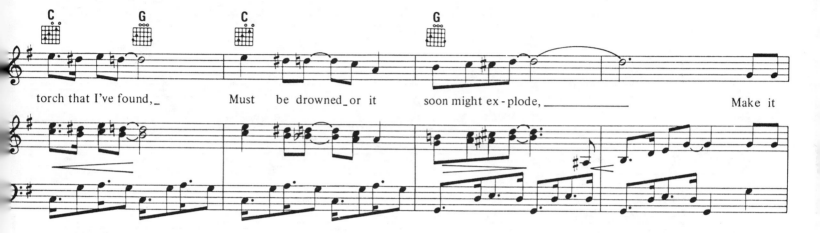

torch that I've found,_ Must be drowned_or it soon might ex-plode,_____ Make it

One For My Ba - by and one more for the road, That long, long road._____

___ It's road._____

EVELINA
(From The Musical Production "Bloomer Girl")

Lyric by E.Y. HARBURG
Music by HAROLD ARLEN

ya gon-na keep de-lay-in' the day.

Don't— ya reck-on it's wrong___ Tri-flin' with A-pril this

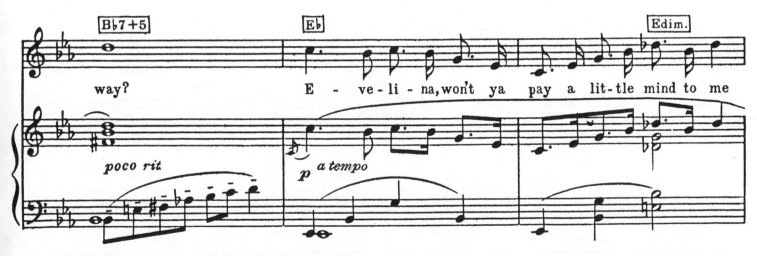

way? E - ve-li-na, won't ya pay a lit-tle mind to me soon?___

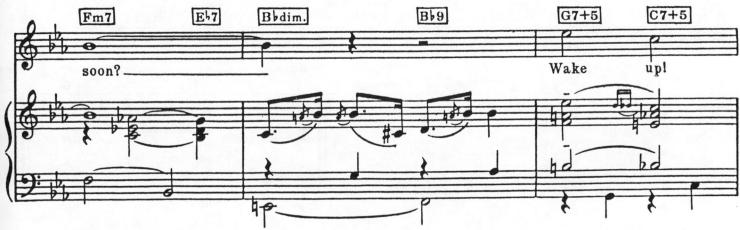

soon?___ Wake up!

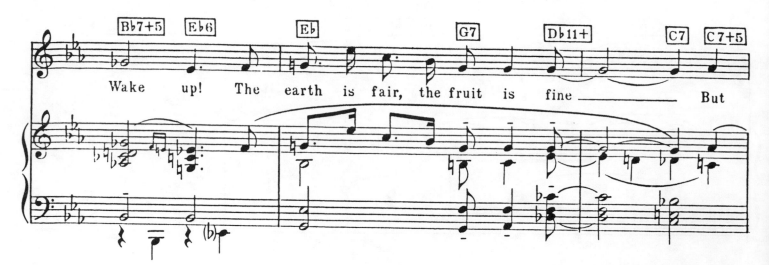

Wake up! The earth is fair, the fruit is fine _____ But

what's the use o' smel-lin' wa-ter mel-on cling-in' to an-oth-er fel-la's

vine? E - ve-li - na, won't ya roll off that vine an' be

mine? mine?

RIGHT AS THE RAIN
(From The Musical Production "Bloomer Girl")

Lyric by E.Y. HARBURG
Music by HAROLD ARLEN

falls from a - bove and fills the world with the bloom of our

love._____ love._____ As

rain must fall and day must dawn, This love, this

love must go on._____

THE EAGLE AND ME
(From The Musical Production "Bloomer Girl")

Lyric by E.Y. HARBURG
Music by HAROLD ARLEN

168

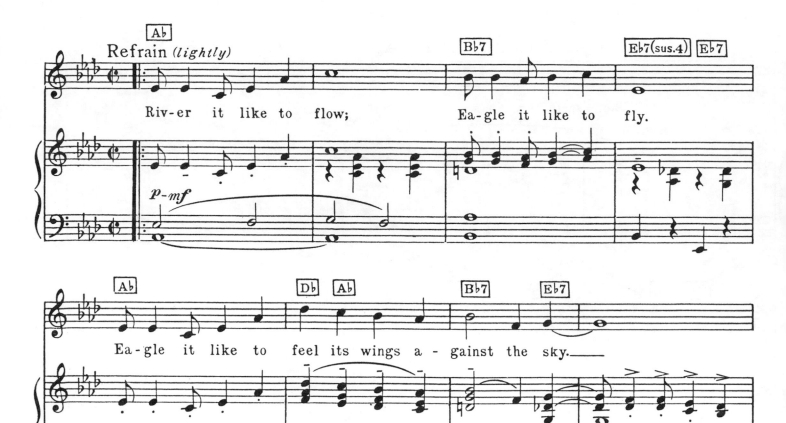

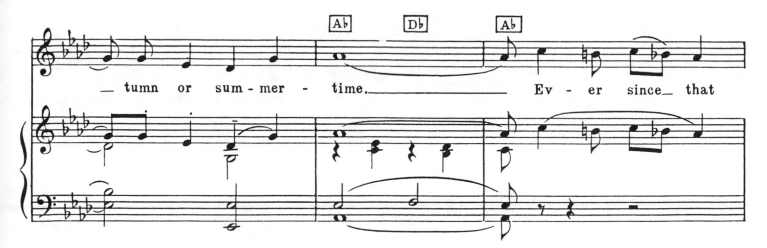

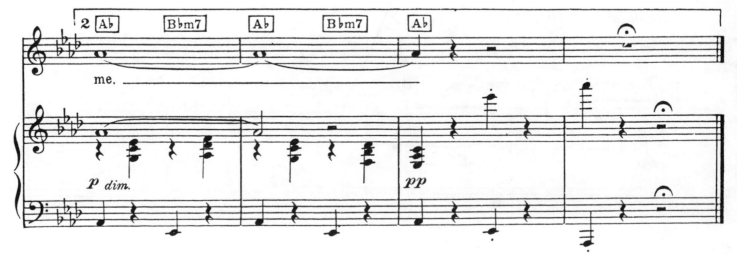

LULLABY
(From The Musical Production "St. Louis Woman")

Lyric by JOHNNY MERCER
Music by HAROLD ARLEN

Slowly

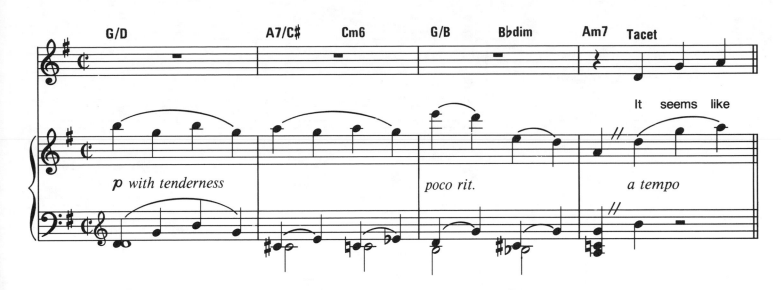

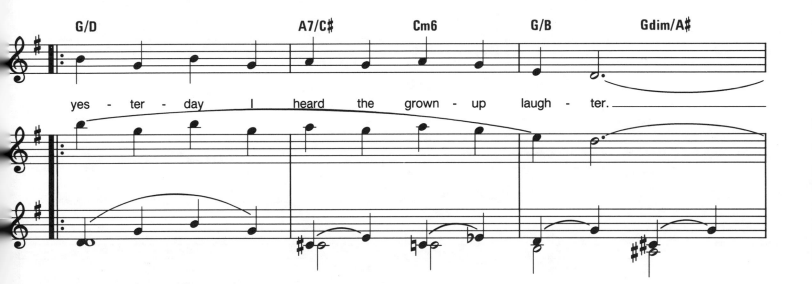

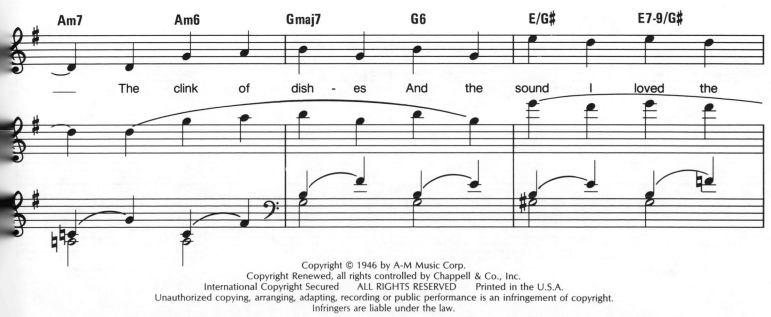

172

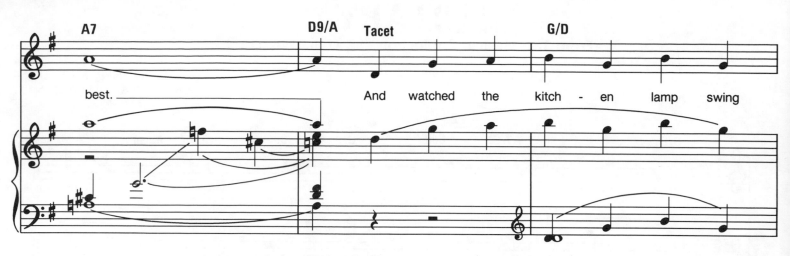

best. _____ And watched the kitch - en lamp swing

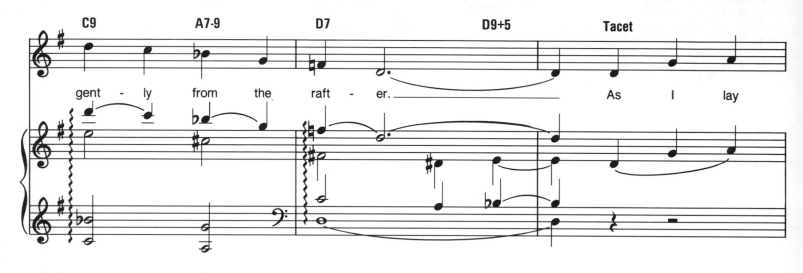

gent - ly from the raft - er. _____ As I lay

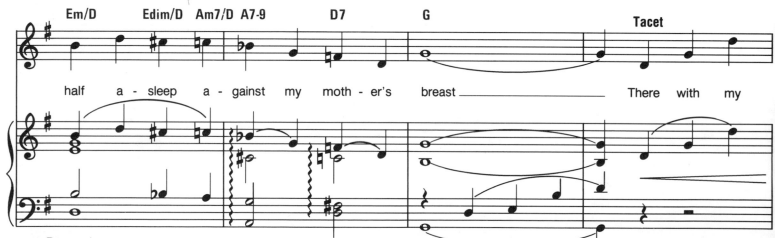

half a - sleep a - gainst my moth - er's breast _____ There with my

Poco piu mosso

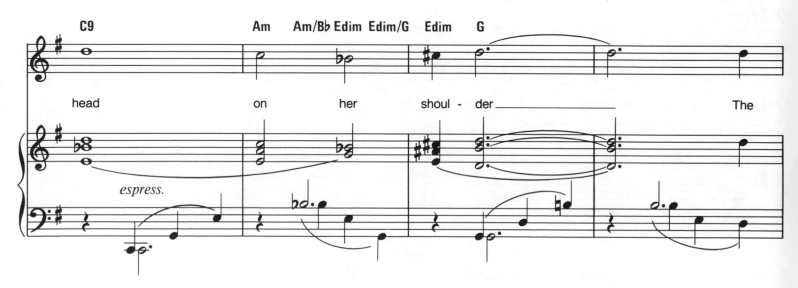

head on her shoul - der _____ The

espress.

wan - na _____ hear my sto - ry _____ Then set - tle back and just sit tight _

While I start re - view - in' the at - ti - tude of do - in'

cantabile

Moderately *(with a steady rock)*

right. _____

very rhythmic

Refrain

Moderately *(with a steady rock)*

You've got to AC-CENT -TCHU-ATE THE POS-I-TIVE, E - lim - my-nate the neg-a-tive,

180

do   Just when ev-'ry-thing looked so dark?_____ "Man," they said, "We bet-ter

AC-CENT - TCHU-ATE THE POS - I-TIVE,   E - lim - my-nate the neg-a-tive,_

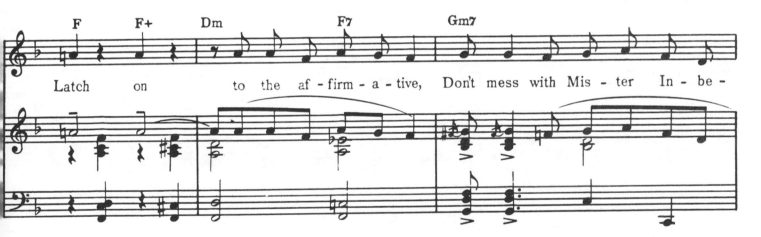

Latch   on   to the af-firm-a-tive, Don't mess with Mis-ter In-be-

tween." No! Don't mess with Mis-ter In-be-tween._ You've got to   tween._

OUT OF THIS WORLD
(From The Motion Picture "Out Of This World")

Lyric by JOHNNY MERCE
Music by HAROLD ARLE

ANY PLACE I HANG MY HAT IS HOME

(From The Musical Production "St. Louis Woman")

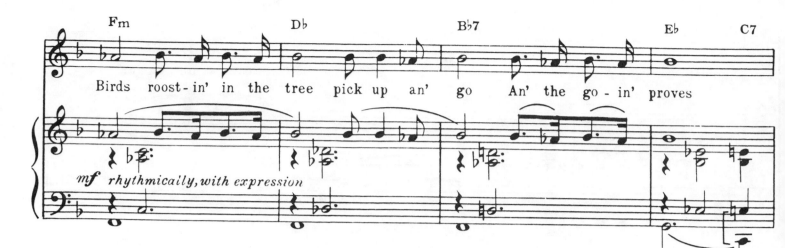

Birds roost-in' in the tree pick up an' go An' the go-in' proves

That's how it ought to be, I pick up too When the spir-it moves me.

Cross__ the riv-er

round the bend,__ How-dy stran-ger, so long friend,__ There's a

voice in the lone - some win' ___ that keeps whis - per - in' roam!

(bravely) C7 Bb Ebm C7 Fdim F#dim C7

I'm go - in' where a wel-come mat is, No mat-ter where that is 'Cause

F Gm Fdim C7 **1.** F

an - y place I hang my hat is home. ___

2. F

home. ___

COME RAIN OR COME SHINE
(From The Musical Production "St. Louis Woman")

Lyric by JOHNNY MERCER
Music by HAROLD ARLEN

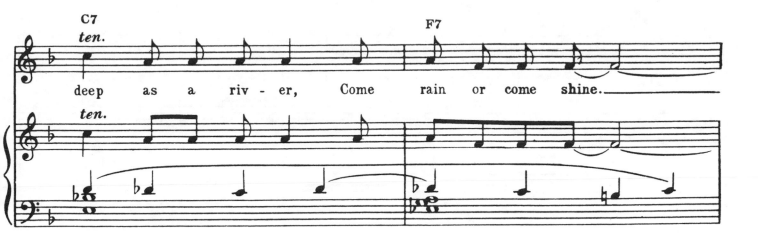

deep as a riv - er, Come rain or come shine._____

I guess when you met me It was

just one of those things, But don't ev - er

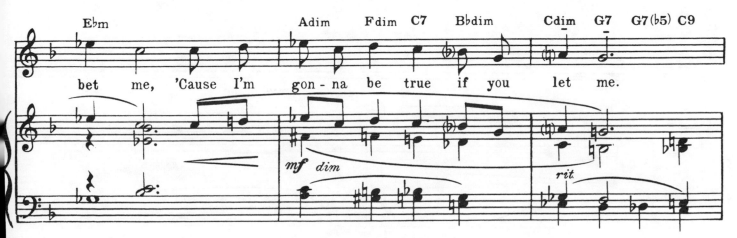

bet me, 'Cause I'm gon - na be true if you let me.

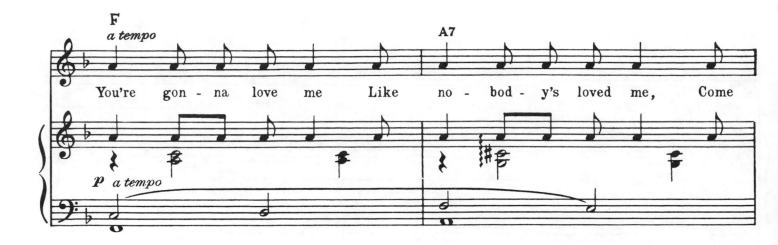

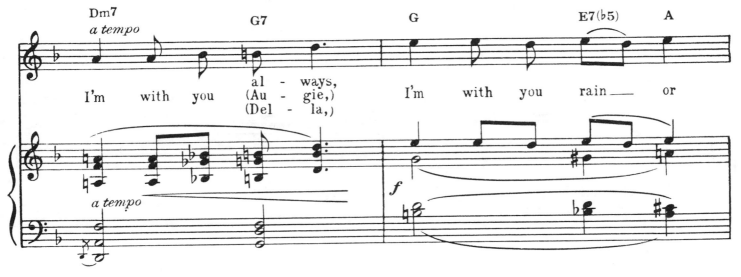

I HAD MYSELF A TRUE LOVE
(From The Musical Production "St. Louis Woman")

Lyric by JOHNNY MERCER
Music by HAROLD ARLEN

Slowly and with tenderness

I had my-self a true love, a true love who was some-thin' to see.

I had my-self a true love, at least that's what I kept on tell-in' me, _____ The

195

first thing in the morn-in'___ I still try to think up a

way ___ to be with him, Some part of the eve-nin' An'

that's the way I live thru the day.___ She had her-self a true love,___ But

steadily

now he's gone an' left her for good.___ The

Lord knows I done heard those back-yard whis-pers go-in' 'round the neigh-bor-

hood.   There may— be a lot of

things I miss,   a   lot of things I don't know, but I   do know this:

Now I ain' got no love an' once up-on a time I had a

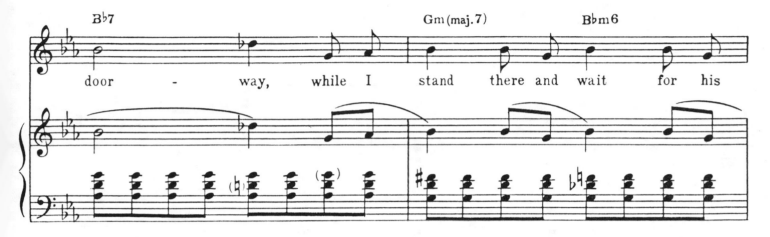

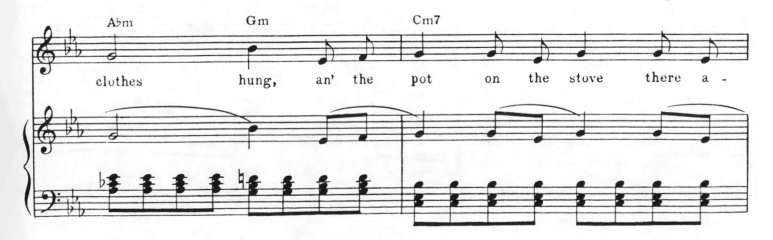

hum-min',_____ Where is he, while I watch the ris-in' moon?_____ With that

gal in that damn ol' sa-loon?_____

No! _____ That ain' the way that it

used to be. No! _____

199

A WOMAN'S PREROGATIVE
(From The Musical Production "St. Louis Woman")

Lyric by JOHNNY MERCER
Music by HAROLD ARLEN

1. I don't know who it was wrote it, or by whose pen
   it was signed. Some-one once said and I quote it: "It's a
   wo-man's pre-rog-a-tive to change___ her mind."

2. An-y fruit, e-ven a lem-on, should have a beau-
   ti-ful rind. But if that lem-on's a lem-on, It's a
   wo-man's pre-rog-a-tive to change___ her mind.

He may have you in a hal - ter___
If he won't bow from the cen - ter,

Har - nessed be - fore___ and be - hind. But till you
And you're po - lite - ly in - clined; If he won't

kneel at that al - ter, It's a wo - man's pre - rog - a - tive to
rise when you en - ter, It's a wo - man's pre - rog - a - tive to

change___ her mind.
change___ her mind.

Prom - ise
They say

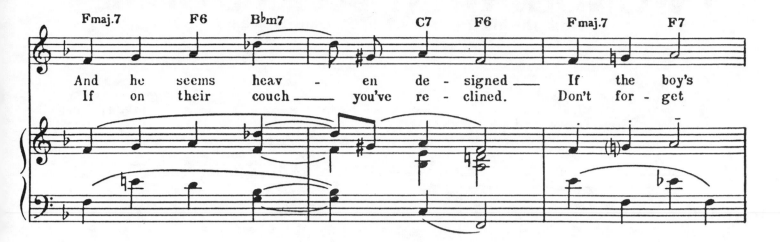

And he seems heav - en de - signed ___ If the boy's
If on their couch ___ you've re - clined. Don't for - get

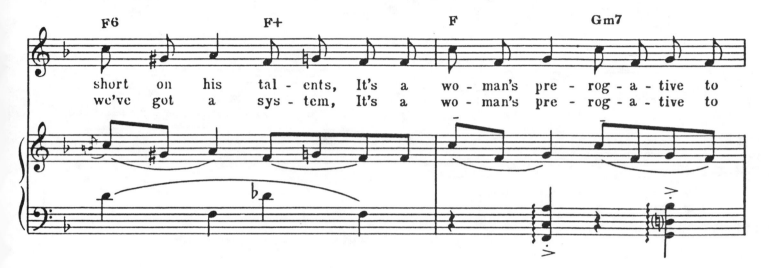

short on his tal - ents, It's a wo - man's pre - rog - a - tive to
we've got a sys - tem, It's a wo - man's pre - rog - a - tive to

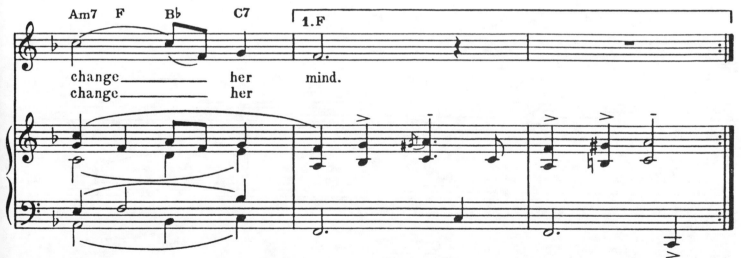

change ___ her mind.
change ___ her

mind.

I WONDER WHAT BECAME OF ME

(From The Musical Production "St. Louis Woman")

Lyric by JOHNNY MERCER
Music by HAROLD ARLEN

Lights___ are bright,___ Pi - a - nos mak - ing mu - sic all the

night ___ And they pour cham - pagne___ just like

it was rain. It's a sight to see, But I

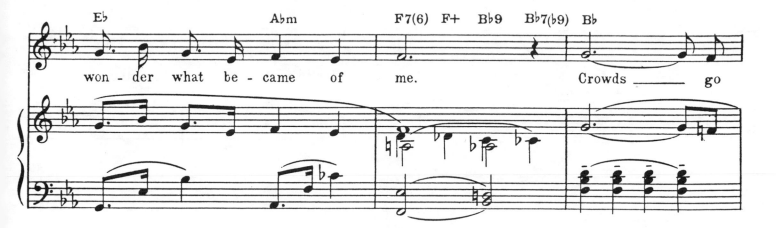

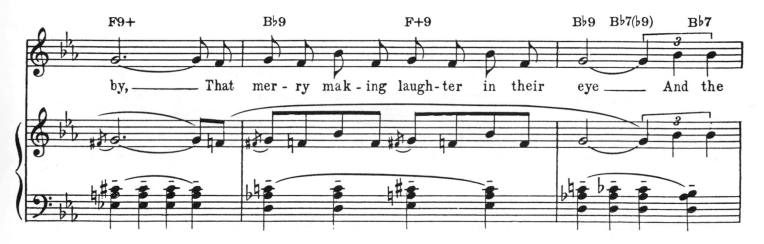

way___ Some-thing went a - stray And I can't ex - plain, It's the

same cham - pagne, It's a sight to see But I won-der what be-came of

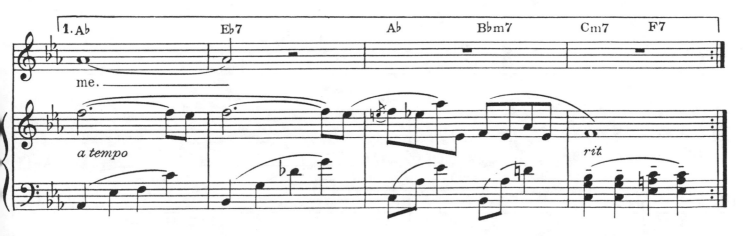

me.___

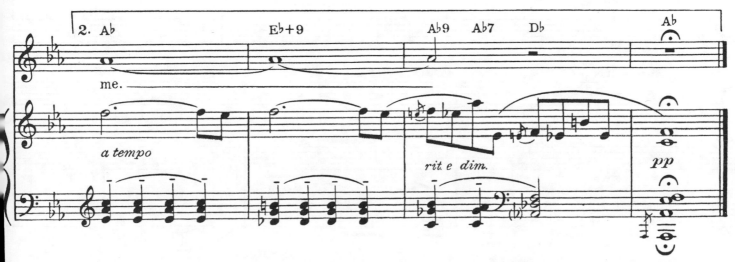

me.___

IT WAS WRITTEN IN THE STARS

(From The Motion Picture "Casbah")

Lyric by LEO ROBIN
Music by HAROLD ARLEN

Now sud-den-ly I know____ You are the one.____

Here,____ as in a day-dream, By my

side you stand; Here____ with my to-mor-rows in your

hand.____ It was writ-ten high a-bove That I

have to have your love Or I'll ne-ver be free. And

HOORAY FOR LOVE
(From The Motion Picture "Casbah")

Lyric by LEO ROBIN
Music by HAROLD ARLEN

Very Moderately

Verse

Here's to my best ro-mance, Here's to my worst ro-mance,

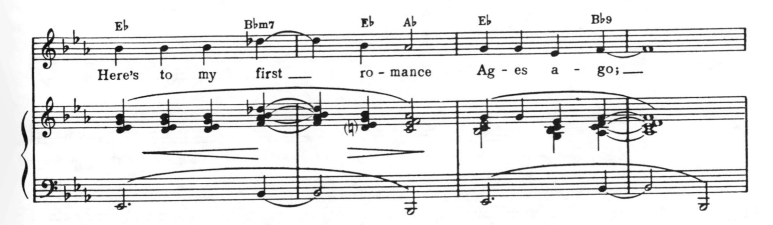

Here's to my first ro-mance Ag-es a-go; Here's to the girls I've kissed And to com-plete the list,

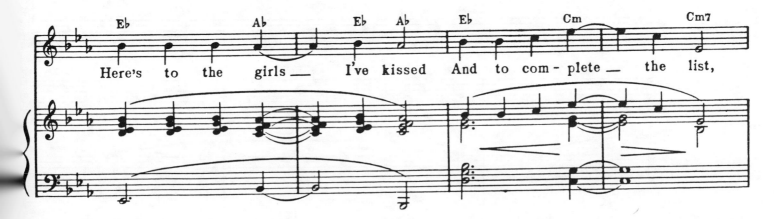

FOR EVERY MAN THERE'S A WOMAN

(From The Motion Picture "Casbah")

Lyric by LEO ROBIN
Music by HAROLD ARLEN

FOR EV-'RY MAN THERE'S A WO-MAN, For ev-'ry life there's a plan___ And

wise men know it was ev-er so; Since the world be-gan

Wo-man was made for man.__ {Where is she, where is the wo-man for me?} For
{Where is he where is the lov-er for me?}

WHAT'S GOOD ABOUT GOODBYE?
(From The Motion Picture "Casbah")

Lyric by LEO ROBIN
Music by HAROLD ARLEN

WHO WILL IT BE
WHEN THE TIME COMES?

(From The Motion Picture "Down Among The Sheltering Palms")

Tune Ukulele A D F♯ B

Lyric by HAROLD ARLEN and RALPH BLANE
Music by HAROLD ARLEN

TODAY I LOVE EV'RYBODY
(From The Motion Picture "The Farmer Takes A Wife")

Tune Ukulele
A D F# B

Lyric by DOROTHY FIELDS
Music by HAROLD ARLEN

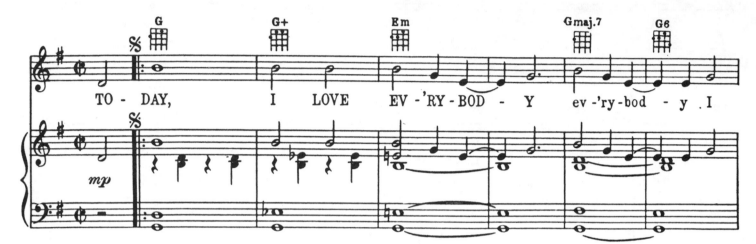

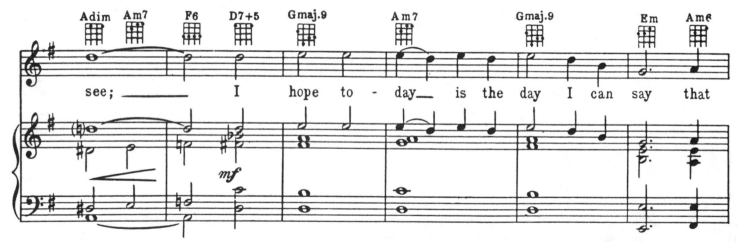

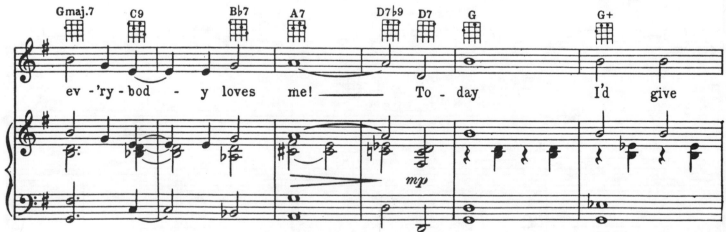

WITH THE SUN WARM UPON ME

(From The Motion Picture "The Farmer Takes A Wife")

Tune Ukelele
A D F# B

Lyric by DOROTHY FIELDS
Music by HAROLD ARLEN

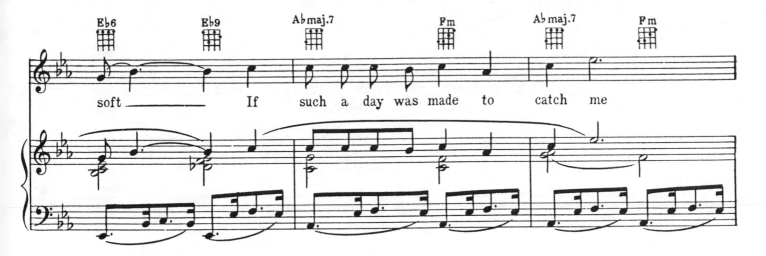

soft _____ If such a day was made to catch me

then I'm caught. I'm caught by the thirst-y bees By the

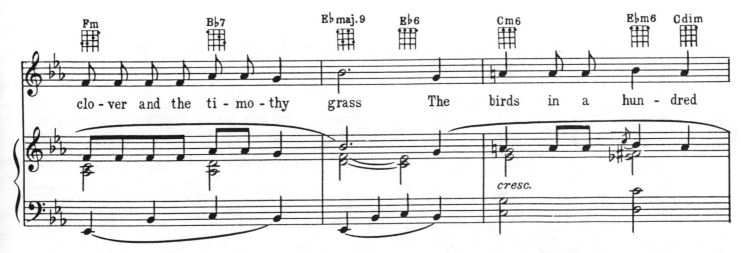

clo-ver and the ti-mo-thy grass The birds in a hun-dred

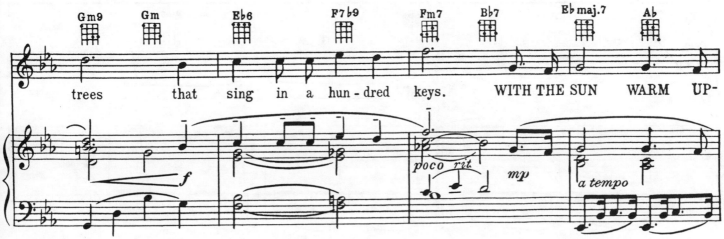

trees that sing in a hun-dred keys. WITH THE SUN WARM UP-

HOUSE OF FLOWERS
(From The Musical Production "House Of Flowers")

Lyric by TRUMAN CAPOTE and HAROLD ARLEN
Music by HAROLD ARLEN

Tune Uke
A D F# B

Very moderately

ROYAL: My house is made of flow-ers,___ the warm winds car-pet the floor.___

When-ev-er there's spring show-ers___ I o-pen a rain-bow door___ The

frog, the toad, the tur-tle_ make my home their home.___ My

cur-tains are crepe myr-tle, and the fire - flies fly neath my dome.___

I've nev-er had mon- ey and I'll

nev - er need none, the moon is my lamp and my clock is the sun. My home's a home for

THE MAN THAT GOT AWAY

(From The Motion Picture "A Star Is Born")

Lyric by IRA GERSHWIN
Music by HAROLD ARLEN

DISSERTATION ON THE STATE OF BLISS
(LOVE AND LEARN)
(From The Motion Picture "The Country Girl")

Lyric by IRA GERSHWIN
Music by HAROLD ARLEN

A SLEEPIN' BEE

(From The Musical Production "House Of Flowers")

Lyric by TRUMAN CAPOTE
and HAROLD ARLEN
Music by HAROLD ARLEN

When you're in love and you are won-d'rin', if he real-ly is the one. There's an an-cient sign sure to tell__ you if your search is o-ver and done. Catch a bee and if he don't sting you, you're in a

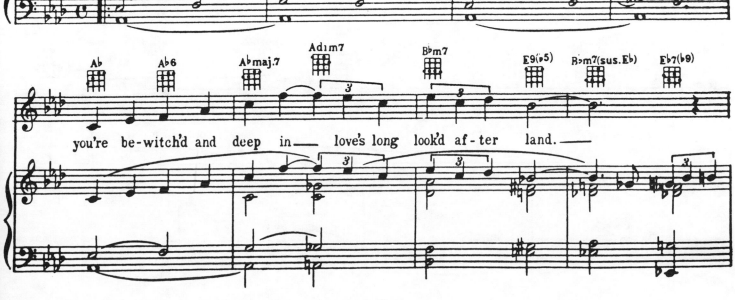

242

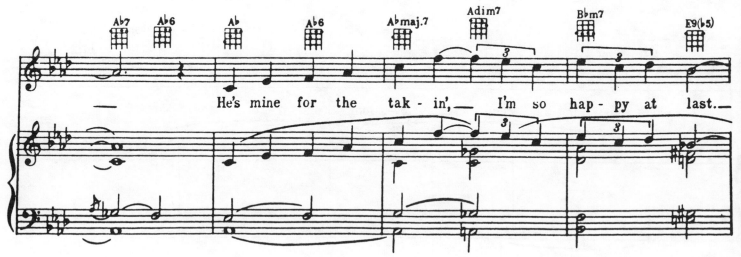

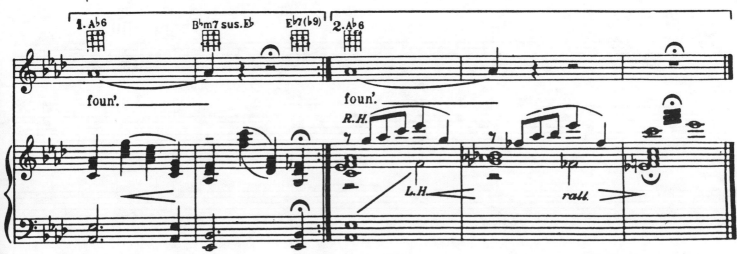

I NEVER HAS SEEN SNOW

(From The Musical Production "House Of Flowers")

Lyric by TRUMAN CAPOTE and HAROLD ARLEN
Music by HAROLD ARLEN

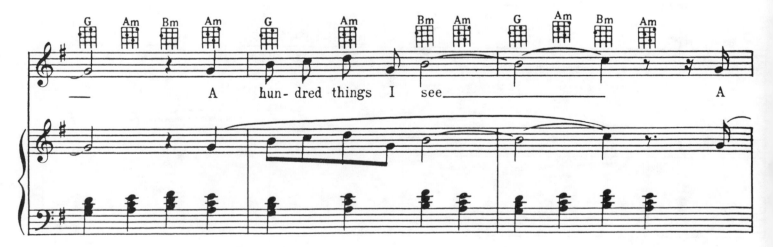

247

When I laid my eyes on that near to me boy/gal with that far a-way look,__ and

right from the start,__ I saw a new hor - i - zon and a

road to take me where I want - ed to be took,

need - ed to be took, __ and

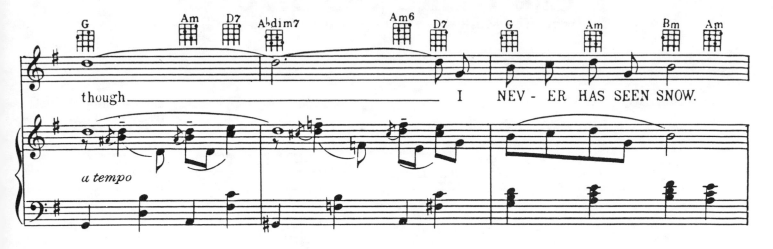

though_____ I NEV - ER HAS SEEN SNOW.

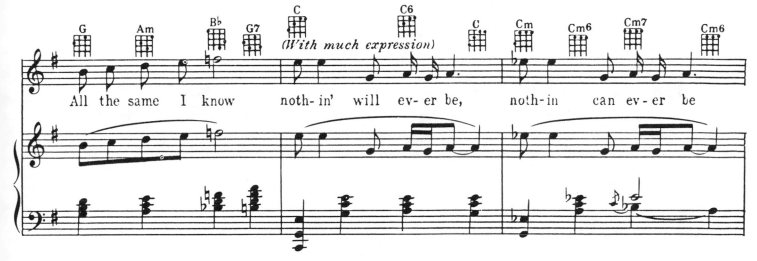

(With much expression)

All the same I know noth-in' will ev-er be, noth-in can ev-er be

beau - ti - ful as my love is, like my love is to me._____

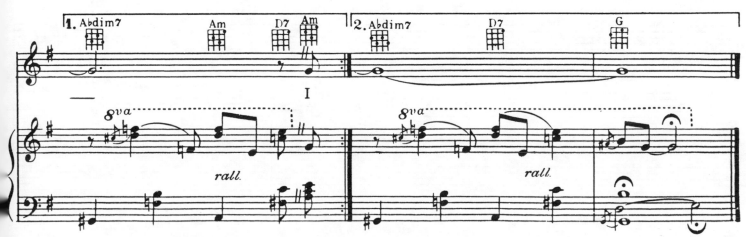

I

DON'T LIKE GOODBYES

(From The Musical Production "House Of Flowers")

Lyric by TRUMAN CAPOTE and HAROLD ARLEN
Music by HAROLD ARLEN

DON'T LIKE GOOD-BYES, tears or sighs, I'm not too good at leav-in' time.

I got no taste for griev-in' time. No, no not me.

You've been my near one's, Al-ways my dear one's, I nev-er thought that

I would find_ An-oth-er love, a dif-f'rent kind,_ But it came to be._ *rhythmically*

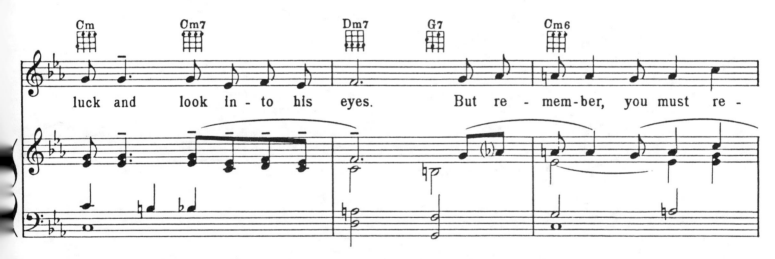

Well, if you think I'm tell - ing you lies, Go try your luck and look in - to his eyes. But re - mem-ber, you must re -

mem-ber he's mine,_ And my world o - ver-head has a clear new shine._ *cresc.*

Don't want to leave you, sor-ry to grieve you,

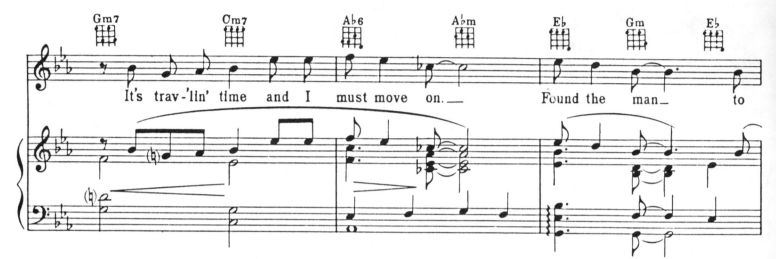

It's trav-'lin' time and I must move on.— Found the man— to

lean up-on,— And if I could ar-range it, Oh, would I care to change it, Not

Segue to Interlude

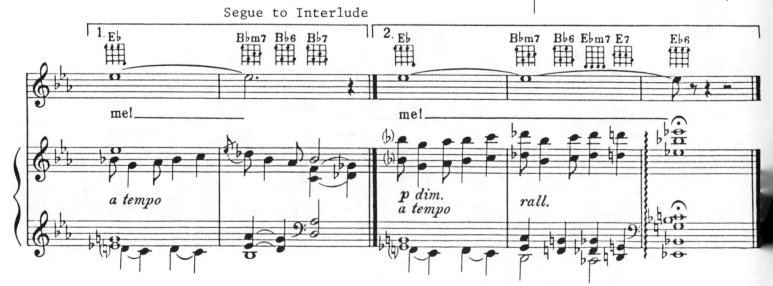

me!_____ me!_____

Interlude

COCOANUT SWEET
(From The Musical Production "Jamaica")

Lyric by E.Y. HARBURG
Music by HAROLD ARLEN

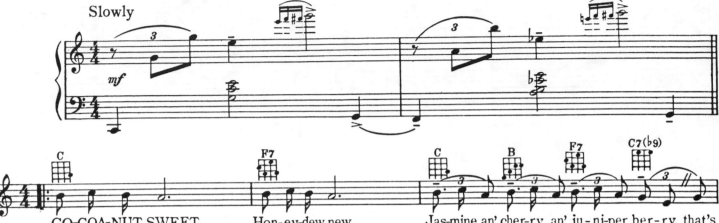

CO-COA-NUT SWEET   Hon-ey-dew new   Jas-mine an' cher-ry an' ju-ni-per ber-ry, that's

you.   CO - COA - NUT SWEET   But-ter-cup true

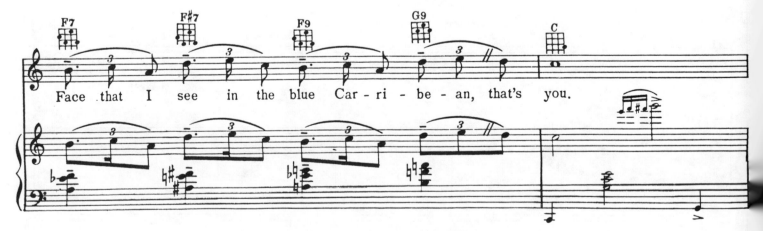

Face that I see in the blue Car-ri-be-an, that's you.

LITTLE DROPS OF RAIN
(From The Motion Picture "Gay Purr-ee")

Lyric by E.Y. HARBURG
Music by HAROLD ARLEN

*Symbols for Guitar, Diagrams for Ukulele.

Refrain *(tender and childlike)*

Nev - er let a min - ute lie there on the shelf, For there may be

in it all of life it - self.
1. Lit - tle smiles of hope,
2. LIT - TLE DROPS OF RAIN,
3. Lit - tle thoughts of love,

Lit - tle drops of tears, Make this thing called love go danc - ing down the
Lit - tle rays of sun, Make the hope - ful rain - bow glow for ev - 'ry-
From each tongue and pen, Make for peace on earth and all good will to

years.
one.

men.

PUSH DE BUTTON
(From The Musical Production "Jamaica")

Lyric by E.Y. HARBURG
Music by HAROLD ARLEN

THERE'S A SWEET WIND BLOWIN' MY WAY

Lyric by E.Y. HARBURG
Music by HAROLD ARLEN

Richly, with an easy pulse

There's A Sweet Wind Blow-in' My Way _____ Blow-in'

love and kiss-es from hill an' tree _____ Blow-in' con-grat-u-la-tions

_____ from all the world to me _____ It's blow-in' my

GOOSE NEVER BE A PEACOCK
(From The Musical Production "Saratoga")

Lyric by JOHNNY MERCER
Music by HAROLD ARLEN

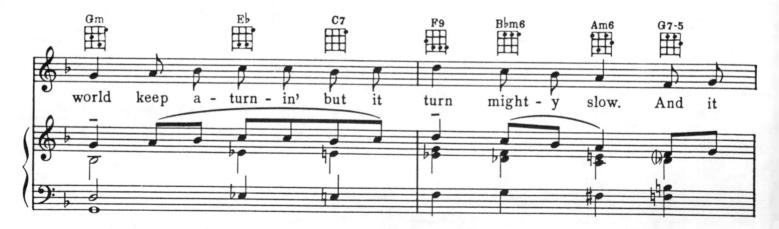

*Symbols for Guitar, Diagrams for Ukulele.

things gon - na stay the way they be - gan.

Refrain *(Freely - with great sensitivity)*

F' in - stance, GOOSE NEV - ER BE A PEA - COCK, Don't I

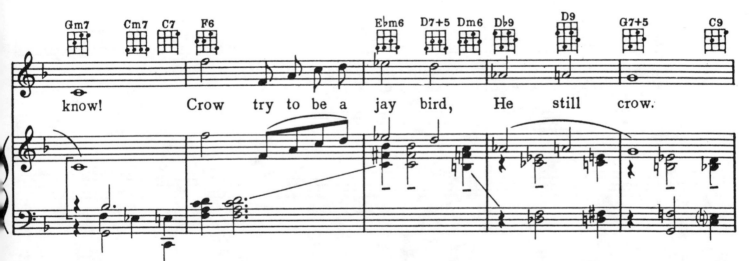

know! Crow try to be a jay bird, He still crow.

Bust his cack - le in two, still can't sing,

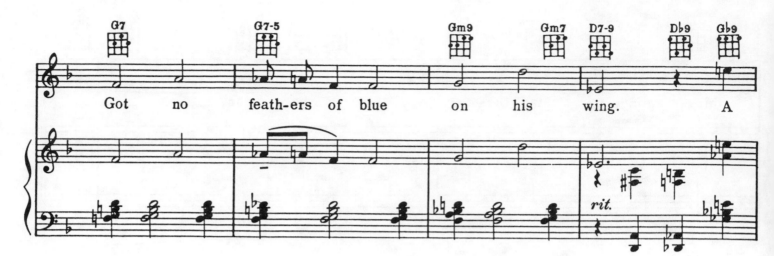

Got no feath-ers of blue on his wing. A

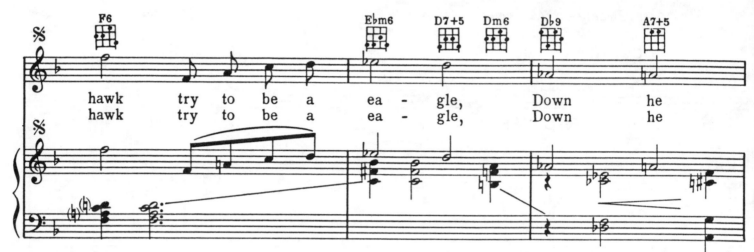

hawk try to be a ea - gle, Down he
hawk try to be a ea - gle, Down he

fall, So don't walk a - round all big - ge - ty like, or
fall, Dere ain't nev - er been too man - y fine birds a -

To Coda

squinch - i - fy up too small; 'Cause may - be you is the
set - tin' up on de wall; And may - be you is de

rit.

ver-y best you of all! _____ Be proud of who you is And what you

do, No mat-ter where you is, Act dat way too.

And ev-'ry - one you see be proud of you. Re-mem - ber

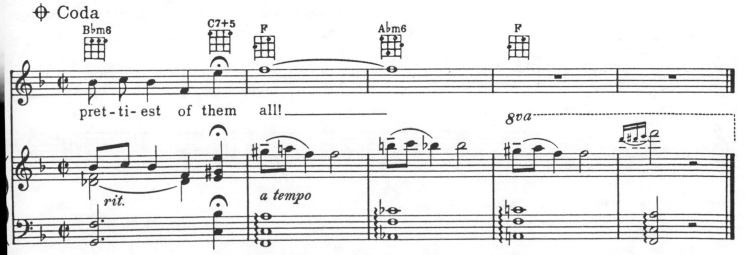

pret-ti-est of them all! _____

PARIS IS A LONELY TOWN
(From The Motion Picture "Gay Purr-ee")

Tune Uke
G C E A

Lyric by E.Y. HARBURG
Music by HAROLD ARLEN

*Symbols for Guitar, Diagrams for Ukulele.

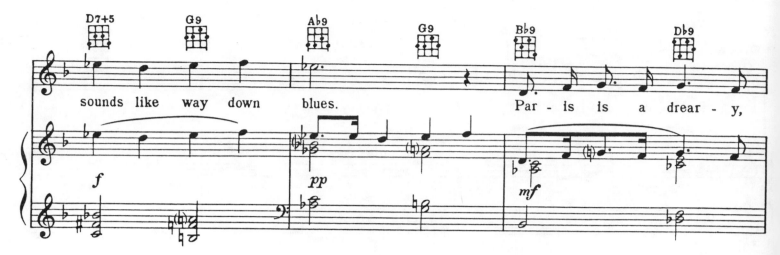

chim-ney's moan, the riv - er cries, each glam-or-ous bridge is a bridge of sighs;

a tempo

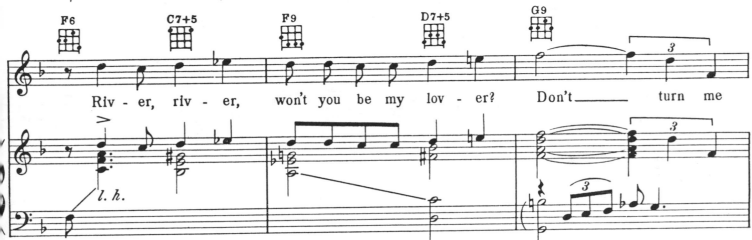

Riv - er, riv - er, won't you be my lov - er? Don't_____ turn me

l. h.

down   For Par - is   is such a lone - ly,   lone - ly

sfz   *rit.*

town.

pp a tempo   *dim.*   *pp*

THE MONEY CAT
(From The Motion Picture "Gay Purr-ee")

Lyric by E.Y. HARBURG
Music by HAROLD ARLEN

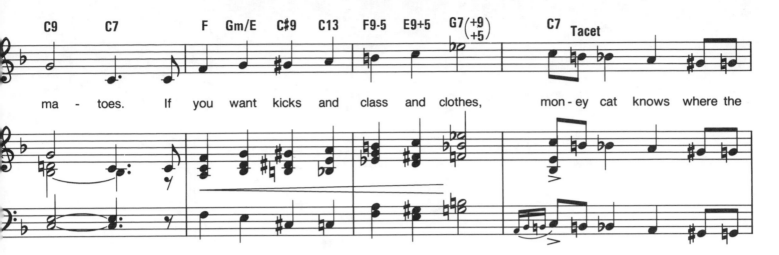

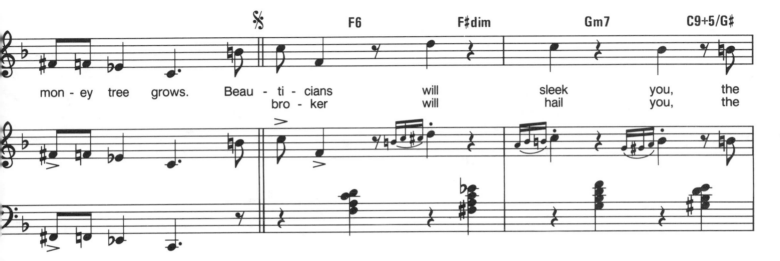

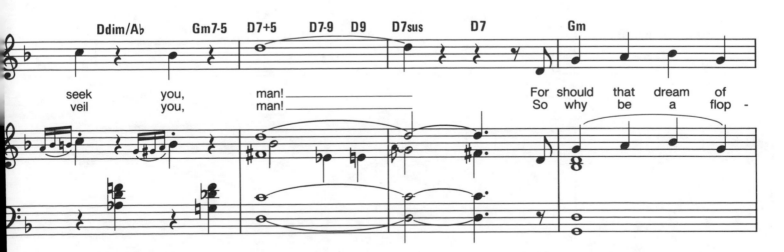

Am7   D7(-9 +5)   D9   Gm   D7+5/Ab   D7+5   G13   Gm7

glor - y   be   part   of   your   plan,   if   an - y - one   can
o - la   with   egg   on   your   pan,   if   an - y - one   can

Cm7   C7   C9   F   **To Coda**   F13/A   E13/G   F13/A   Bb13

help   you,   the   mon - ey   cat   can.
save   you,   the   mon - ey   cat   can.

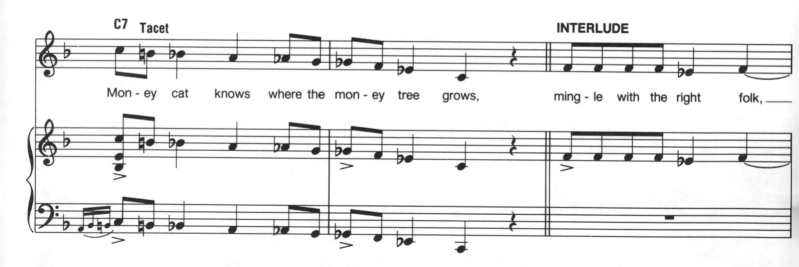

C7   **Tacet**   **INTERLUDE**

Mon - ey   cat   knows   where   the   mon - ey   tree   grows,   ming - le   with   the   right   folk,

Adim/Eb   G#dim/D   Adim/Eb **Tacet**   Adim/Eb   G#dim/D   Adim/Eb **Tacet**

meet   the   bot - tle   pop - pers, ___   rub   el - bows   with   the   e - lite ___

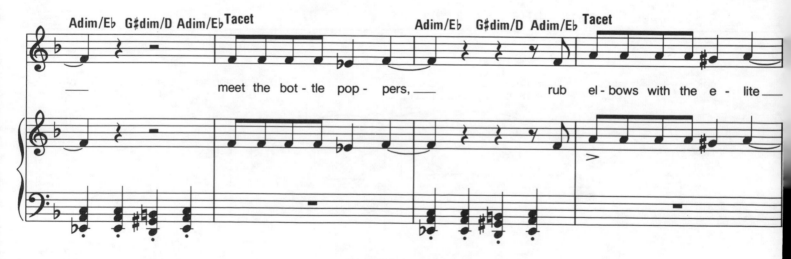

Mon - ey cat can buy up____ an - y - one who's high up.____

We've got dicks and pol - i - tics and law____

in the palm of our paw.

The

D.S. al Coda

CODA

THAT'S A FINE KIND O' FREEDOM

Lyric by MARTIN CHARNIN
Music by HAROLD ARLEN

HAPPY WITH THE BLUES

With a gentle nod to ED JABLONSKI — author of the
biography of HAROLD ARLEN "HAPPY WITH THE BLUES"

Lyric by PEGGY LEE
Music by HAROLD ARLEN

*Symbols for Guitar, Diagrams for Ukulele.

THE MORNING AFTER

Tune Uke
A D F♯ B

Lyric by DORY LANGDON
Music by HAROLD ARLEN

With Spirit

Piano

Verse

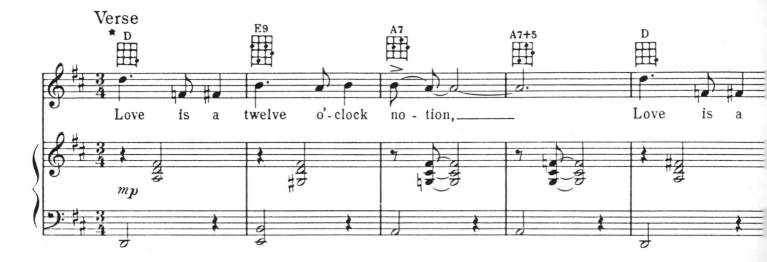

Love is a twelve o'-clock no - tion,____ Love is a

bed - time po - tion;____ Love's a laugh in the night, a

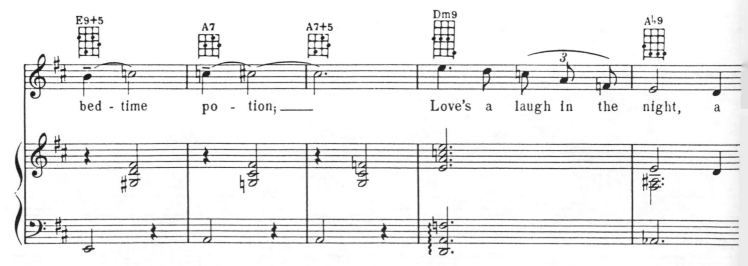

Symbols for Guitar, Diagrams for Ukulele

sun-down de - light.　　　　　　　　　　Just a laugh in the

night and then the fun's up,____　　Then the fun's up,____

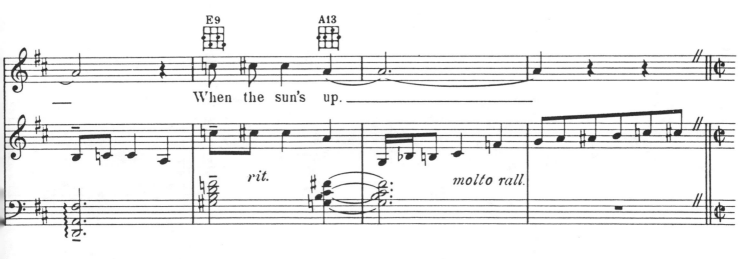

— When the sun's up._____

Chorus-Sensitively

If I did-n't have to　face THE MORN-ING AFT - ER,____

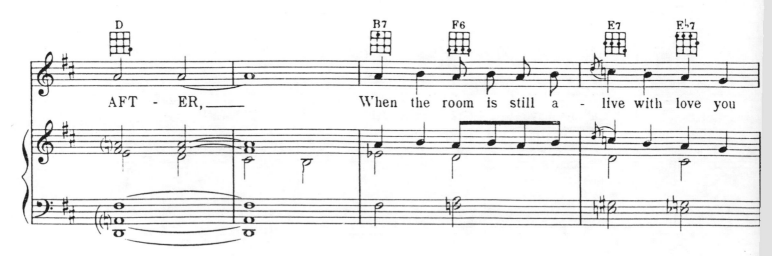

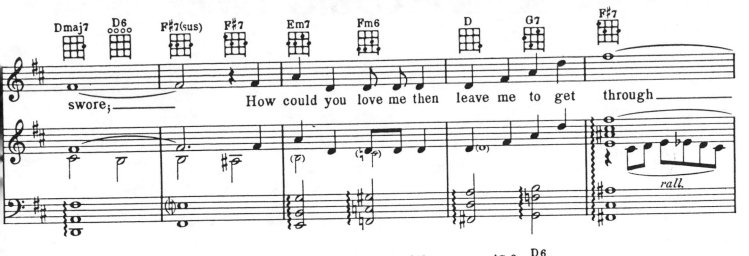

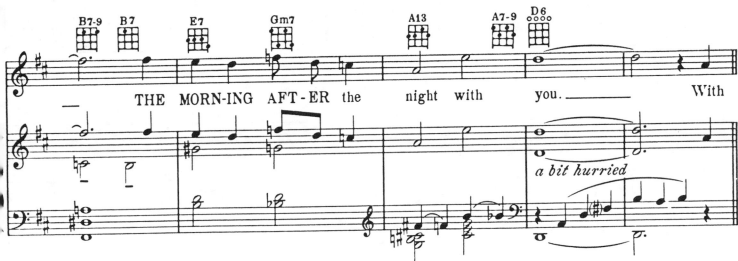

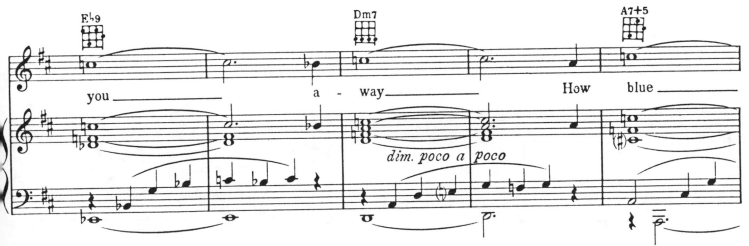

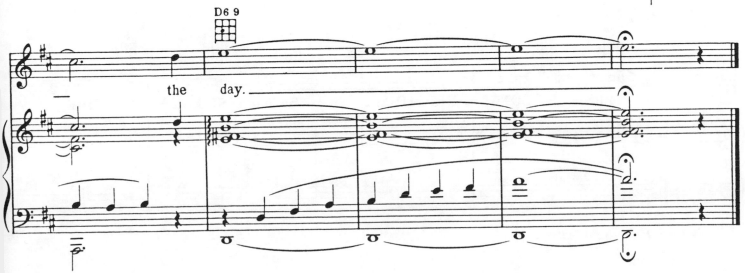

SO LONG, BIG TIME!

Lyric by DORY LANGDON
Music by HAROLD ARLEN

*Symbols and Diagrams for Guitar.

THE SILENT SPRING

Lyric by E.Y. HARBURG
Music by HAROLD ARLEN

I HAD A LOVE ONCE

Lyric and Music by
HAROLD ARLEN

In A Pensive Mood

I had a love once;

I had a love once.

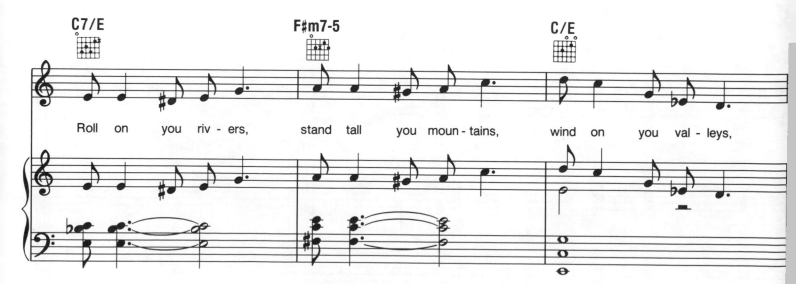

Roll on you riv - ers, stand tall you moun - tains, wind on you val - leys,

PROMISE ME NOT TO LOVE ME

Lyric by E.Y. HARBURG
Music by HAROLD ARLEN

Freely, with tenderness

Pro - mise me not ___ to love me or a - dore me for a

life - time. Pro - mise me not ___ to waste a sin - gle sigh on one good -

bye. Love is by far ___ too bit - ter sweet for hearts that beat too

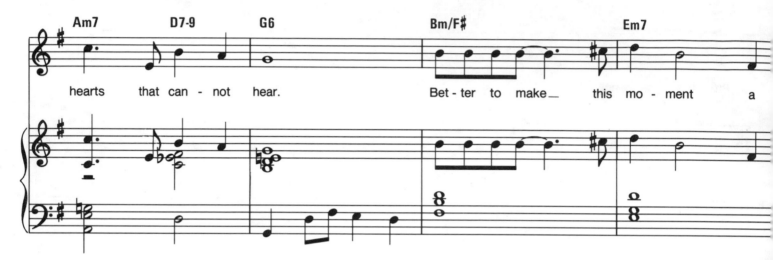

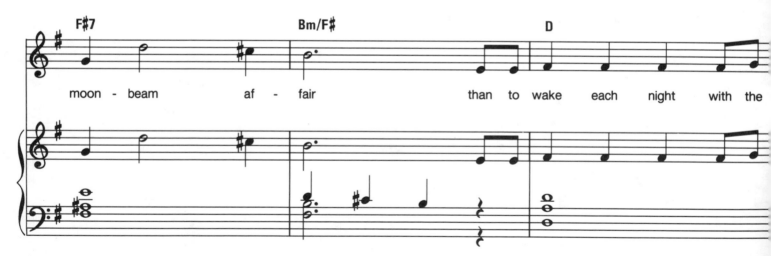

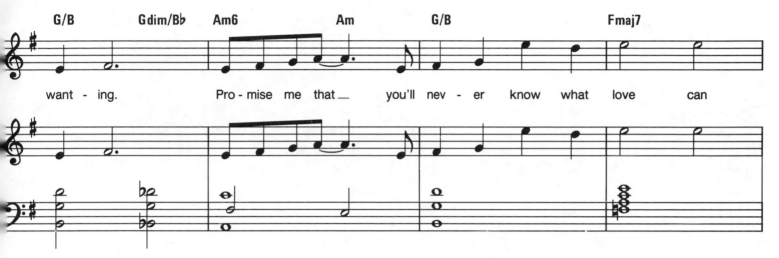

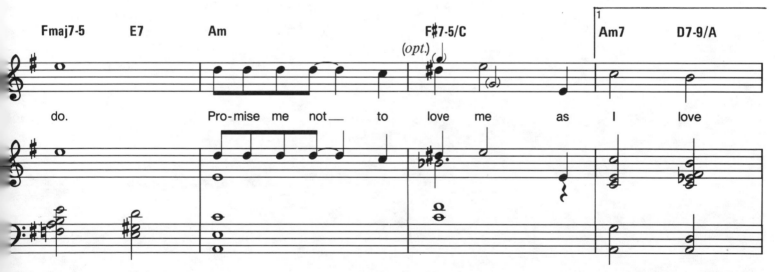

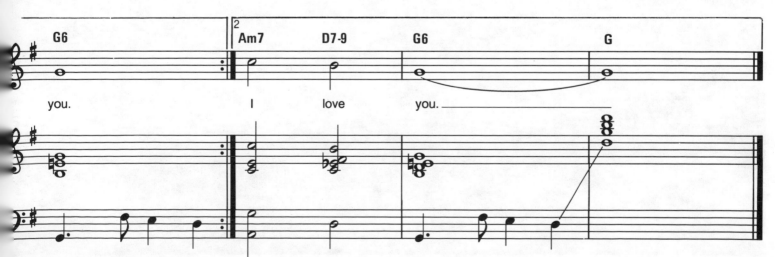

Harold Arlen and his wife, Anya, in Hollywood, 1935